AN ACCIDENTAL
JUBILEE

Artist's impression

AN
ACCIDENTAL
JUBILEE

*

ALICE
WARRENDER

*

STONE TROUGH
BOOKS

JUBILEE
Pilgrimage to Rome
(to obtain an indulgence
in the R. C. Church)

TO MY PARENTS

ISBN 978 0 9544542 6 5

Published by Stone Trough Books
The Old Rectory, Settrington, York
YO17 8NP

✳

C O N T E N T S

Prologue—Scotland—England
France—Switzerland—Italy

✳

I L L U S T R A T I O N S

PROLOGUE

*

19TH FEBRUARY 2011. Our world was turned upside down this morning by one of those telephone calls one never wants to get.

Breakfast was late, although I had been up early to make it. Jack wanted to film Geordie coming into our bedroom and kissing me goodbye, as if it were a workday, for his documentary on Noonan Syndrome. It was fun: Geordie finds it hard to pout his lips and kiss one, so trying to teach him made us all laugh. Grandma who likes the routine of bacon, tomato and fried bread every day of the week was already downstairs. Just as I was carrying the coffee to the table, the telephone rang and a voice asked to speak to Fiona Warrender. Did I know what the situation was with my twenty-eight year old daughter Alice?

Helen, the nurse on the telephone, told me that Alice had come off her bicycle at eleven o'clock last night and had been taken to Chelsea and Westminster Hospital. 'This morning we gave her a CT head scan, which has shown a blood clot between her brain and her skull. She is fully conscious, a bit muddled, but able to give us your telephone number. We are transferring her to the neurological department at St Mary's Paddington and it is likely that she will have to have surgery. Is there anyone in London who could come to be with her?'

I asked politely whether we should have a second opinion. 'No,' she said, 'there is no time.'

Only at that moment did I fully realise how serious things were. I said to Helen, 'I'm quite robust, is there anything else at all we should know?' There was a fraction of a second's delay before she said, 'Just get here as soon as you can.'

By this time Johnny was by my side absorbing the situation. He suggested we ring his brother Michael, whose wife Oki is Alice's godmother. Thank goodness they were there. They could not have been sweeter or more helpful and Michael went straight to the hospital. Jack and I drove together to Glasgow and by the skin of my teeth I caught a flight to Heathrow and got the Paddington Express, arriving here at 15:00.

As I arrived Michael had just been told that Alice was out of the operating theatre and that we should be called up to the Major Trauma Unit on the ninth floor in an hour's time. We sat having a cup of coffee together as he told me what he knew.

When he arrived at Chelsea and Westminster, Alice was so pleased to see him that there were some tears, but she said she felt fine, apart from a cracking headache. It seems that after dinner and drinks with friends in St James's she had left, characteristically, without saying goodbye, so as to avoid being persuaded to go on to a club. She has no memory of what happened next and all we know is that while paramedics were attending to a man having a heart attack outside Fulham Broadway station, one of them saw a body and a bicycle sprawled in the middle of the road. Having pulled her to the side they called an ambulance, which recorded that her observations, pulse rate, blood pressure, blood sugar were normal. She stated that she did not wish to go to hospital and wished to be taken home, but they convinced her otherwise owing to her complaining of a sore head. When it was suggested she got into the ambulance she refused to leave her bike on the side of the road. They said 'We never take bikes' and Alice replied 'Well, I'm not getting in then'. Their only hope was to squeeze it in as well.

Without any witnesses or company to take her home, Alice had to remain in Chelsea and Westminster for the rest of the night and after persistently complaining of a sore head she was given a CT head scan in the morning which revealed internal bleeding that had persisted for nine hours.

By the time Michael arrived at the hospital they all knew that they had an emergency on their hands. He accompanied Alice and several medics in an ambulance to St Mary's, reassuring me that amidst the crisis she remained calm and happy. He was told to keep her talking and on no account to let her fall asleep. The surgeon whom Michael met wanted to get on with things straight away. He said that she was extremely fit and in great shape, which was a positive advantage for what he had to do.

This morning's telephone call about 'possible brain surgery' had turned into five-and-a-half hours of our darling daughter in the operating theatre. So far that was all I knew.

Michael would have waited, but this was something I wanted to face alone. I felt extremely calm but still did not know how things would turn out. Writing up my diary, something I have always done, helped me now, because had I thought about what was happening it would have made me feel very frightened. As one hour turned into three and having heard nothing, I took myself up to the 9th floor to see what was going on. Ruth, the nurse, whose name I had been given, was off on her break and a nice enough guy said Alice wasn't up from the recovery ward yet and anyway it would be a bit messy (his very words) and they would need some time to clean her up. Incredible. I have come back down to sit in the reception, which is just a hall with a receptionist behind a desk pushing people in the right direction. It is quiet and not busy which is a relief, but I wish they would come for me.

At last my mobile rang and a voice said I could go up in half an hour. All I wanted was to be with her. I waited for the eternal thirty minutes to pass and then I could go, stand by her bed and reassure her I was there.

As I walked into the Unit, the surgeon, Rob, introduced himself and asked if I would like to see the scan in order to show me what he had done before I saw Alice. There was something wonderfully reassuring about his matter-of-fact, calm manner. It seemed almost as if he were proud of his day's work and wanted to share, in the nicest way, how clever he had been. He explained that he had cut through her head in her hairline, from the top of her right ear to above her left eye. He then showed me an x-ray on the computer of the bleed, a big balloon of white that he had removed. He said it had been a much bigger extradural haematoma than they had realised, and that she was incredibly lucky that her brain had moved to the opposite side of her head and consequently, in the long term, she shouldn't be too badly affected by it. This was as good as news gets.

Alice, lying on her bed plugged into goodness knows how many bits of kit, looked very ill. Her pretty little face smiled at me from under a huge bandage. 'I'm so sorry, Muma' were the first words she said. There were tubes everywhere, up her nose, in her arms and even one out of the top of her head, but she managed to convince me in the short time we had that she was her own self and not some stranger that we would all have to get to know.

JOURNAL

I spent three days barely able to move, drifting in and out of sleep. The pain of my head was relentless. Nothing would dull it and instead I developed the morphine rash of a heroin addict, and this meant more drugs were added to my concoction of pills. During the night a nurse sat by my bed, waking me every three hours to shine a light in my eyes. Continual blood tests caused my arms to become black and blue and so weak I could barely lift them. Gradually over the course of a week my body gained strength. I went from being washed in bed, to sitting in a chair unassisted, to being pushed to a shower—although still too weak to wash myself—and by the end of the week I proved I could walk up a flight of steps unassisted and get through a night of pain without morphine. I was discharged and able to return home to South West Scotland.

Ayrshire. March—April—May—June

The all-consuming role of co-running a three-year-old digital business, my independent London life and enjoyment of long runs along the river, were gone. From day one I was embarking on a two-year recovery, the mental outcome of which was uncertain, and all that could be advised was careful consideration of life ongoing. For three months I spent most of the time asleep. Just having a bath would drain the little energy I had. My head hurt so much I was unable to eat anything that involved chewing and I lived off soup and Calippos. There were trips to London for monthly brain tests and hormone checks, all of which showed a continuous gradual improvement and remarkable recovery from such major surgery. My family nursed me and took it in turns to warm up the armchair in my bedroom and tell me about their day. Instructed not to read or look at a screen, I lived in my imagination. Book tapes gave me company when no one was around and the days passed happily with an inner sense of gratitude for life that I had never felt before.

By May I was enjoying giving a purpose to each day through a new-found passion for painting pictures in Papa's studio. Although I lacked energy for anything more than a thirty-minute walk and was unable to get through a day without sleep, the swelling of my head was going down, the pain was gradually getting less acute and my hair was slowly growing back. When I returned to London for a heart check in mid May I went to Stanford's, the travel bookshop, to buy a map on pilgrim routes to Rome. There was no such thing and the woman helpfully told me that the first English guide book on a route from Canterbury was currently being published and should be on the shelf in September. I left the shop with a heart monitor under my jumper and a strong desire to walk to Rome.

For the next month this was my aim. Secretly I researched the pilgrimage known as the Via Francigena. I ordered the three books published in America that trace the entire route from Canterbury to Rome and were the only current publications in English. With Papa based in France and Muma spending time there keeping him company, it was easy to work at my project alone. I knew that I was in no fit state to walk to Rome but I believed I could get there. Each day I would walk a little further and plan a bit more of the route and it was wonderful to have something to get better for.

My next visit to London was on the 27th of June and I so hoped that at this appointment the doctors would discharge me. In the meantime I talked through my project with Muma and Papa who were both nothing but encouraging and supportive, knowing how important it was for me to have a goal and that it depended on the doctors. From the moment I had the idea I never thought I would not embark on it, so I planned and prepared as if I had the go-ahead. My rucksack was all but packed in my room. I had been wearing-in my new trekking shoes and, apart from writing an outline itinerary for the next three months, I thought very little about the actual journey. I just longed to be on it, independent, alone, and to meet strangers who knew nothing about my head. In my mind, on the 12th of July I was leaving from Canterbury.

I really believed it was my final trip to Charing Cross Hospital. I was full of enthusiasm and excitement. I sat in the narrow corridor, the odd one out amongst stroke victims, the youngest by far — a hollow reminder of how unbelievably lucky I was. I was called in to see Dr. Sharp, the head of the department. I thought this was a sure sign it was my last visit.

There is a look that no words can convey that makes my insides flutter. It says with seeming disbelief, You just do not know how lucky you are. Ever since I opened my eyes on the 9th floor of the Major Trauma Unit, every morning when my bed was surrounded by doctors with clipboards examining me, and now when this man took me through the details and possible long term consequences of my accident, I knew I carried a responsibility for the life I have.

I didn't ask the doctor if I could walk to Rome. I could not hand over the responsibility of the decision. As the appointment progressed I realised I was not going to be discharged; however, the instruction to take more exercise and spend time outside to build up my lack of vitamin D was enough to give me the go-ahead. I expressed my frustration at having to return to my childhood bedroom and said that, if it was O.K. by him, my plan was to go on holiday and do some walking in Europe. He thought that a very good idea and said as I was doing so well we could leave the next appointment until December.

Canterbury – Coldred. July

'Ah! Now I'm giving a tour to these people,' her smile said as she stared at me. Behind stood a small group of expressionless men and women clearly unenthused by their tour guide who was desperately searching for a way to liven them up and leapt at the chance of handing over the introduction to a real-life pilgrim. 'Tell them,' her open hand gesticulated enthusiastically towards the group, 'have you walked far?' I'd just walked through Christ Church Gate to the cloister; my waterproof, although on, was bone dry. A minute earlier she might have asked me to get off the grass when I jumped over a stone wall into the cloister to grab my map which the wind had carried away. With a burst of enthusiasm I confidently addressed the group, 'I am starting today on a pilgrimage to Rome along the Via Francigena, a route following the stages recorded by the 10th Century Archbishop of Canterbury, Sigeric, on his return from Rome.' The tour guide glowed and asked the obvious question. 'No, there's no one else in my group, I'm going alone and I hope to get to Rome in about three months.' I beamed at the group and got no response. With a 'good luck' from the guide I headed out of the Christ Church Gate and turned left down Burgate. I smiled and thought Enough talking about it, I have just got to get on and do it.

I never imagined that I would not enjoy the first day. Leaving home was tearful but I was longing to be free of the past, unencumbered with labels, and with a future ahead of me. I felt elated by being my own responsibility. I was independent, un-fussed and free. It rained a lot. I followed the North Downs Way but came across no other walkers. The people I did pass in villages gave no reply to my smiles and occasional hello. I thought perhaps I would like Kent more if it was not in Britain. When the rain got heavier I sheltered in the Norman church of St Mary at Patrixbourne, which had the most elegant 17th Century Swiss glass engravings framed within stained glass and set as panels in the windows. Dripping wet I carried on to Coldred where I had booked a B&B for the night.

Jackie was a sweetie — perhaps a humbug in a wrapper with red edges. When she said, 'You're not like any of the other pilgrims and don't look the type to walk to Rome,' I did not dare ask her what I did look the type for. I was so pleased to be here. The room was a kit build in the garden and the rain poured down racketing off the flat roof. We agreed breakfast at eight and I said I was happy calling it a day and there was no need to drive me to a pub for dinner.

It was cold; I showered and put on trousers and a hoodie rather than my nighty. My hips were rough from the backpack, and my body was sore; my calves, my soles, my neck, my shoulders were all asking me what an earth I was doing. I sat up, eating the whole jar of bourbon and cream biscuits, drinking tea and watching 'The Night Watch' a film about gay love during World War I. That first night I slept very deeply.

Coldred – Calais. July

I ate breakfast alone, closed into a room, and the door only opened to admit the toast to the table. It did surprise me how impersonal people can be. No questions were asked, no stories told and nothing new learnt. I left as if I had just arrived. I headed out across the rape seed fields. The yellow flowers had passed, the faint smell of honey was gone and the seedpods, pointed at both ends, grazed against my legs as I pushed through the wet overgrown path towards the coast. In Dover Church two men hovered over me asking what I was up to. As drips dropped from my waterproof coat and wet rucksack I told them I was about to get on the ferry to France and walk to Rome. Their only response was concern for me doing it alone. They probably thought I was much younger than I was. I headed for Dover ferry terminal and thought no more of it.

I was very tired and the rain continued to fall so I decided against going on deck to wave goodbye to the white cliffs and instead tucked into mushy peas and lasagne, which combined with a rocky sea made me feel very ill as I padded the pavement of Calais to a dilapidated hotel with the name in neon lights across the roof. The immigrants, tanned men with predatory eyes and wolf whistles, cut short my exploration of the town. Instead I sat at a table pushed up against the window and watched the raindrops snake their way slowly down the pane as I ate 'Chef's special' salad. The colours made it look like lunch regurgitated on a plate, it tasted of nothing; however, it passed some time before I returned to the filthy, bare, building-site of a hotel. The soles of my feet throb and my hips are bruised. It will be the weight of the bag, which can't get lighter until I go further. I am happy to be alone but without anyone else to interrupt them my thoughts run wild and my emotions change rapidly from high to low. It is at times like this that I wish I could take the edge off things and drink till I drown out overactive thought. If I can just stay on the right path and not give in to temptation I wonder where that will take me.

Calais – Licques. July

On day three the pattern of the adventure began to form. I was in the Nord–Pas-de-Calais region of Northern France and I got to Guines where I had planned to stay, only to find out it was Bastille Day and everything bar a medieval museum was closed. It being my first day in France and wanting to leave Calais far behind me, I was keen to keep going but first I knew I must secure a bed for the night. With no accommodation listed in my guidebook I went to make friends with the woman behind the desk in the museum. Despite the obvious language barrier she could not have been more willing to help me. I named a village that I ambitiously wanted to get to, and from behind her computer she made several telephone calls. Eventually as a last resort she called the campsite despite my not having a tent. There she assured me the owner would give me a bed in a caravan for one night. I had two packets of crisps in my bag, which was bad planning, as I never imagined how hungry I could get. It continued to rain and I worried that the first of my three guidebooks was not going to get me to Besançon. As well as the importance of eating a bigger breakfast and carrying more food I also learnt that I could not rely solely on the directions in my guidebook and, when I was lost, the basic map provided per day was very limited and did not help me.

Turn right then sharp left to skirt the woods along a narrow grassy track was the direction written in the book. Even with the compass reading and the kilometre scale I had no idea how far I had come or how to relate my position to a page of directions. Unable to see anything other than vast ploughed fields I came to the conclusion that the wood must have been felled and the path gone. I got out my road map which was too large-scale to help with a cross-country route but together with it and a compass I knew I could get myself to the village of Licques along the minor roads. As the rain beat down I bent my hooded head right over and studied the map rather too close to my face. Compass in hand I confidently trudged up the edge of a field drowning in its own mud as I headed towards where I thought the road was. Of course had there been a single car I would have seen the road but I was swiftly learning that this part of France had very few people and even fewer cars. With a great relief I came to the road and followed it all the way to Licques.

Tomorrow I would work out my walking speed so that I should be able to cross-reference my timing and compass-readings with the directions in the guidebook. Allowing for my faster pace when unsure of the way, I calculated 6 kilometres per hour and when calculating how many hours of the day would be spent walking, including breaks, I worked on 5 kilometres per hour. How essential this strategy became to my journey.

Licques was a splurge of houses and not a shop in sight. Having lit a large candle in the huge empty stone church and said a prayer for my night ahead, I took the first road heading out of the village in the hopes it would be the right end of town for the campsite. I arrived with that feeling of having taken an unusual amount of exercise and been hungry for so long that it didn't really matter if I ate now or in several hours. A warm, smiley, brown Frenchman was sitting behind the desk in the reception hut of Le Camping des Trois Pays. He welcomed me, stamped my pilgrim passport[1] for the first time in France and insisted on carrying my bag. As we wound our way through his campsite past loos, showers and a swimming pool, he 'beuffed' at the weight of my bag. Embarrassed by the thought in his mind of a strong broad woman I blushed and agreed. We got to the smallest caravan I have ever seen with a thick pale blue stripe around its waist. It is like a home, all mine. I began to feel the cocoon of my own world forming. I passed so much today, leaving a city down a

---

[1] This passport gives proof that the holder is a pilgrim and ideally must be stamped in each place of rest (see endpapers).

dreary canal, making a friend in the only village I passed through, and learning how it really feels to be lost and alone. I am so happy.

After a delicious burger and an ice cream on a stick in an empty room by the swimming pool it finally stopped raining, so I sat in a collapsible canvas green chair facing my room for the night and painted it. A well fed young Norwegian girl stood by my side throughout, apart from a dash back to her mobile home to spray herself with scent that got up my nose and made me think of her innocence and if only she knew what the thrill of smelling good for other people could lead to. Tucked up under several rugs listening to 'Fingal's Cave' fill the space in the caravan, I wished, for the first time, I had someone next to me.

Licques – Wisque. July

I woke feeling uncertain. A place that was such a relief to get to and could quickly be turned into my own and give me warmth, comfort and security now had to be left behind. It was an empty feeling: uprooting, repacking and heading off as if blindfold to somewhere which might be better, worse, or just as good.

It continued to pour with rain and I could not believe that the overgrown and stinging hedgerows of this morning were right, but somehow I ended up in the village in the book and once again felt so lucky that things were going my way. I joined a tarmac road, which accentuated the pain in my soles; however, not going wrong on a road almost annuls the pain. I stopped for lunch behind a tree in a lay-by and a huge ham and cheese baguette hot from the morning's sun went down before I could taste it. How relieved I was that the woman gossiping in the boulangerie early this morning had come across my stick on the floor before I had gone over the crest of the hill.

Another day had almost passed without seeing anyone. I was walking through a hamlet with that great feeling of knowing that the next stop for the night is not far away when a woman rushed out of her house and offered me a whole lot of drinks at top speed. 'Café,' I said without a thought and in I went to her house. I learned French at school but there the only things I really learned were recreational. Anything taught in a classroom—with white boards, textbooks, and a system to be conformed to—just put me off. There was too much fun to be had breaking petty rules and instead I got by on last-minute cramming for exams. In the long term this has meant that I retained very little. My French is poor but I do know quite a few words and, although I can't string a string a sentence together, I can talk briefly about a lot of different things. When two people speak very little of each other's language it is surprising how much you end up understanding through tone, expression and hand gesture. In this house I met three children from the woman's first marriage, her first husband having died, one child from her second marriage (to an English man, Lloyd, from whom she is now divorced), her sister-in-law who was married to her brother who is now dead, two dogs and a cat. The woman could not have been more all over me, however the rest of the family were uninterested. Perhaps they had pilgrims coming through their door daily and were fed up with yet another. However, I doubted this was really the case as I was yet to see one or even someone just exercising their dog.

I drank several cups of coffee, something I learnt the French always have bubbling away in a glass-heated jug on the kitchen counter. I shared my problem of finding a place to stay for tomorrow night. Out came a telephone directory and several telephone calls were made. Unable to help, my hostess became rather insistent about me spending two nights here. I thanked her but refused. Having turned down food, shower and now a bed it was time to leave before I became rude. She forced the point of how brave I was, which I brushed off for fear of thinking too much about what she really meant. She gave me ten euros and after much miming and finally a drawing I understood it was for me to light four candles for her children and one for me. I walked on with bags of energy and the pain of my soles lost in the comfort of strangers.

On the hill up to the Abbey in Wisque a little girl and her bruiser of a dog walked with me side by side. We both got the giggles, as she didn't understand a word I said. If the dog had not got so puffed by the hill I would have walked ahead but instead, as it gasped for air, I floated in the atmosphere of two people walking close enough to be friends.

L'Abbaye de Notre Dame was huge. I was looking forward to it as it was the first 'religious accommodation' on the journey and I had never stayed in something described like that before. I knew Italy had religious accommodation throughout so I was intrigued to see what I was in for. It was an austere, neo-gothic building sprung up behind a high wall with little space in front of it other than for a few cars to park and a tree surrounded by a patch of grass. The Abbey was straight ahead with no obvious door, just a long level corridor with a door at either end. I went through the one on the left and peered down the gloomy long corridor. It was silent, there was no doorbell, and having half-shouted half-said 'Bonjour' I got no reply. I headed down the corridor to reach the entrance at the other end, where there were steps leading to a large oak door. Without opening it I put my ear to the door and heard that recognisable high-pitched Gregorian chant in which each nun seems to sing the words of the Latin Psalm just slightly out of time with their neighbour. I went to collapse on the bit of lawn under the tree and cringed at the smell I gave off.

Having sat for nearly an hour I caught the flutter of a black habit through the open door and headed in again. Sister Luce had a smile so big it was as if she had met me before. We walked to a cottage in the garden, dilapidated but full of character; warped floor boards, a sitting room with sunken floral patterned furniture fading with the curtains, a kitchen of tin crockery once contemporary now fit for camping, one bathroom and my room which was a huge space looking out through wooden shutters down the garden and on to the cobalt blue horizon. I had the choice of two high beds, both with warm rugs to go over my sleeping bag. We had dinner in a small room within the main Abbey. The food was terrible—stale bread, packaged cheese, watery soup with floating vegetables and pots of cold custard—but having learnt to eat when food is offered if unsure whether this may happen again, I ate as much as I could bear. There were two other guests at dinner. I tried to break the silence round the table but my stories were too elaborate to translate and I was left laughing to myself while they looked on confused. Sister Luce came to stand over us, eager to join in. She had a glint in her eye and if only I had spoken French we could have got some energy into the room. The silence engulfed us all until Sister Luce's petticoat suddenly slipped to her ankles. She erupted into laughter and the tears welled in her eyes. It was wonderful and I laughed and laughed, the infectiousness of it spreading to the rather more composed guests. By the time we had washed up, dried and gone to evening prayer I thought there was nothing that would keep me awake. But, from within the smelly dense rugs came endless mosquitoes which buzzed and bit all night long. If only they had gone for places easier to itch than between the shoulder blades I might have got slightly more sleep than I did.

Wisque – Thérouanne. July

Since it was the first place in France that I had sat down to breakfast, I was plunged into the confusion by their table-laying. It is not really the laying—very little of that goes on—but rather how to eat in a polite manner with such limited cutlery and crockery. A basic priority for the Frenchman, it seems, is to keep washing-up to a minimum. It is therefore no surprise that ratatouille is a traditional dish. With an unhelpful guest only shaking her head as I pulled things out of the cupboard, I finally narrowed it down to no table-mat, one bowl and a knife. The other cups, saucers, side plates and table-mats seemed to be there solely to fill the cupboards. Cereal was eaten in the bowl before coffee, and a long baguette was cut directly on the table and eaten from the table where a table-mat would have been. This etiquette saved me from many future breakfast blunders. It was the spreading and eating of bread directly from the table that I found hardest to adjust to, but drinking coffee from a bowl, in large greedy gulps was a much better way..

I left not knowing where I was going to spend the night. It rained so hard and the wind blew as if trying to knock me over. I sheltered under a chestnut tree and rang Muma to help me find a bed in Thérouanne, the next village and the only realistic destination in this weather. Muma's French is near perfect and I suggested, with the Internet, she tried to track down the Town Mayor. With my telephone in my inside pocket I carried on, cold and wet, until I came to a roadside café. The shutters were being wound up and three drunks were tripping through the door as I followed them in. I drank two cups of coffee watching the flies get stuck to the ring marks on the table before Muma rang back. I was to meet the mayor in Thérouanne church at 6pm. It was 9am but this place was not fit to stay in much longer. One of three men at the bar at which I had been talking while he smiled and topped up his alcohol levels, kindly paid for my coffee. I took down the address of the place and said I would send a postcard from Rome. On I went to Thérouanne whose streets were gushing with water. I entered the first bar I came to and sat in the back room while six hours passed. The harmless man behind the bar understood I was hungry and brought me a plate of food from what I suppose was his house out the back. I wrote a long letter home on several paper tablemats and for the whole day not one other person came in. Time was up and I headed for the church.

Inside l'Église de Saint-Martin I sat on a pew totally absorbed in the magnitude of the interior until a man bending down to my head height caught my eye line. I leapt up and with little conversation followed him and his wife across the car park to a neglected cottage exterior. Up the incredibly slippery steps they let me in to a cold building and bare hallway. To the left was a door with a sign saying *Salle de Mariage*. The Mayor, a short man with pure white hair with not a strand out of place, pushed the door open and a waft of aftershave caught on the draught as his wife planted her firm figure inside, saying nothing but wearing an expression of concern. The room was filled with rows of plastic chairs all facing the large window onto the street. The other three walls had cabinets filled with chalices and trophies. I thanked them with great enthusiasm in the hope they would at least bring me a pillow. We said goodbye and, having written down their address, I agreed to drop the key off at eight o'clock tomorrow morning.

I piled up three lines of chairs to make space for my bed and went to have a look round. There was one other door off the entrance hallway which led to a bare room with desks doubled up on each other, beyond this was a cold china loo and basin. I had remembered to collect napkins in both places I stopped today so the loo paper store was well on its way. Back outside my room there was a narrow wooden staircase. Up here were two rooms directly above the ones below. They were empty except for a chest of drawers. Inside it were several altar covers, which I pulled out and rolled under my arm. They did little to disguise the firmness of a tiled stone floor but hopefully they would make it slightly warmer. Under the stairs I found what looked like very thin nylon hairnets. I took a handful and stuffed them into my sleeping bag cover to make a pillow. Laying out all my belongings on a table I tried to make the room feel a bit more like home. Not wanting to spend too much time in my bedroom before I had to, I went to the supermarket and ate dinner in the room next door whilst staring through the net curtain at the rain in the car park. Supermarket shopping for one person for one night is an art which took me several weeks to master. At this stage I was still buying four-packs of yoghurts, a whole lettuce, a wedge of cheese, far too much ham and enough chocolate chip cookies for a week.

I have never been someone who can know inside when I have had enough. I just don't get full and it is only afterwards when it is a struggle to sit up that I know perhaps I have eaten too much. It is the same with alcohol. I just can't not have more and if I think that this may be the last drink then I will drink it even quicker so as to make sure there is time for another. The outcome of being drunk never works as a deterrent. Therefore, supermarket shopping for one is fatal, as I just see no enjoyment in rationing the goods and saving some for tomorrow. I curled up on the floor next door with a tummy that felt as if it might pop and fell fast asleep.

Thérouanne - Amettes. July

Thérouanne is a medieval city and feels juxtaposed to the present century. The houses are full of people but the life doesn't spread out into the streets. I happily left it behind and went to ring the Mayor's bell. In I went for breakfast off the table and coffee in a bowl served by his sullen-faced wife tightly wrapped in her dressing-gown. They lived in a well-to-do house and have four children of their own no longer living at home. It would have been a much cosier night in their house. The friendly proud Mayor gave me a map of his town, a leaflet on the history and a piece of paper, which he laid down in front of me. As I read 'Alice, un très bon pèlerinage sur la Via Francigena', he took out a pen and signed it, *Alain Chevalier, Maire de Thérouanne,* in a very official manner which I found particularly uncomforting. I longed for his wife to throw her arms around me and give me a big hug but instead they suggested I use their telephone and call Muma, which then made me want to be having tea in bed with her and Papa.

Despite sleeping well I felt exhausted. My soles ached, my head was heavy and the rain weighed me down even more. Soon I would realise that my routine was not suited to the amount of sleep that my head cried out for, but right now I was still living on the energy of being alone and free from the concern of people who knew what I had been through. So far I had moved further, stayed awake longer and achieved more than I had done since the 19th of February and it brought back the confidence I had lost over the last five months.

I arrived at a farmhouse gîte in the farming village of Ammettes by mid-afternoon. It was Sunday and I had not passed a single shop to buy food in but I was too tired to mind and as soon as Madame showed me to a room in the rafters across the yard I had a hot shower and slept for hours. I woke dizzy with hunger and pulled on some tracksuit bottoms before descending the very steep wooden ladder back into the yard. An old man in worn dungarees smiled at me from behind a mini tractor. I went over and shook his hand. Rubbing my tummy I said in poor French 'I'm hungry' he pointed to a blue door next to mine and amongst what he said I made out the time: seven o'clock. I retreated back to my room to find my watch on the side table. It was ten past seven. I wasn't quite sure what to do but without thinking about it too much I went back outside to knock on the blue door. Madame answered and a rub of my tummy sent her scurrying back inside. She returned with a plate piled high of bread, potatoes, tomatoes, rice, tuna, pate, cauliflower and sweet corn. Standing on her doorstep I would have never guessed what was coming. It lifted my spirits for the first time all day. No sooner had I got back to my room than she knocked on the door and handed me a plate with a slice of chocolate cake and a large jam roll. I had food, plenty more hours of sleeping and an excitement about getting to a big city tomorrow.

Pretty much everyone I have met so far looks at me and says, 'You're brave,' and about two-thirds of them follow that up with 'C'est dangereux.' Then they go on and ask 'Vous timide?' My answer is 'Non'. If I were afraid I would not be doing it. Part of me wants to ask what I should be afraid of but I think I would rather discover it than be told what it is that lies ahead which makes people's eyes alarmingly round and direct.

Amettes - Bruay-la-Buissière July

I walked through rain all the way to Bruay-la-Buissière. It is an ex-coalmining town approached through slums, generic council houses, opencast mines, gypsies and rough men with evil eyes. I was too afraid to go into the bushes for a pee for fear of being followed. The further towards the centre I went the more the pavements became covered in glass. The main town was haunted by the remnants of a huge fête. There were juggernauts with intimidating drivers blocking the streets. I drew unwanted attention on an empty pavement and even the smiling clowns on the lorries seemed to know something I didn't. Thérouanne, Amettes and now this place, all belonging to one of the most fought-over regions of Europe, have an historically corrupt air to them. There seem to be a lot of unsettled spirits around and I really don't like it.

Once in the centre I left the empty pavement to ask for direction to the hotel I had pre-booked. As the queue built up behind me, the woman at the post office counter told me Hotel Le Cottage was two kilometres north of the centre. Very incoherently I asked about the possibility of a hotel south of the centre. Before the conversation got too confusing the next lady in the queue came forward and said in good English that she would drive me to the hotel. As I waited for her to put stamps on her parcel I found myself nearly dropping off against the photocopier. She had to prod me with her elbow as she headed out the door with the parcel in her hands. I put my bag in the boot and could hardly get my seatbelt on before their West Highland Terrier was on my knee warming up my cold skin. As her husband drove I became mesmerised by the speed. Somehow, thankfully, my eye caught the sign on the front of a building, which read *Le Cottage*. 'C'est ici!' I exclaimed and at the next side road they dropped me out. I padded back on very sore feet up the busy highway to a hideous wooden panelled hotel. It looked shut but I pushed open the swing door into a dark reception where there was an older man, a young girl and a baby. I could not work out who was related to whom but they did not look the types for chatting. I was in room Number 1, the restaurant was closed and I was given a code to get in and out of the fire escape so that they did not have to sit at reception. The room was entirely practical, that is without a hint of comfort. There was no lock on the door and the only window opened onto the main road. As I was on the ground floor I put up with a hot airless room rather than risk an intruder. Despite the pain of my soles I needed to find food, so, following the signs down the highway to an industrial estate, I ended up in a café eating a soggy croque-monsieur and drinking fizzy water.

Back in my room with a plastic door wedge firmly in the inside of the closed door, I decided that for my own safety I would bypass the one city ahead that the guide book described as *a former railway hub with limited choice in accommodation and of this some is very poor.* Right now I still had to get out of the city I was in and the safest way, I thought, would be to leave early in the morning.

Bruay-la-Buissière – Arras. July

This was a good plan as at 6am the streets were bare. As I got to the outskirts I passed a few lonely down and outs with universal glazed expressions but certain I could outrun them, even with a heavy rucksack, they didn't frighten me. I was headed for Arras, another city but one renowned for its cathedral and therefore drawing tourists and wealth in equal measure. A distance of 35 kilometres and little time to rest due to the rain, it was my longest day yet and by the time I got to the carbon-stained gothic façade of the *maison diocésaine* my feet and shins were unbelievably sore. Only when the woman showing me to my room was at the other end of the corridor before I had barely moved two steps from the lift did I realise quite how slowly and tenderly I was taking each step.

Getting in to this building amused me. It is on a busy street and I stood facing the huge wooden door pressing the buzzer several times before I finally realised the door was open. Inside it is like a modern cloister with long arched corridors off each corner. Neither of the two women behind the glass-fronted reception spoke anything other than very rapid French. My room is basic and cold but has two beds, which means two pillows and two rugs. The refectory in the basement has no windows and space for about 200 people but only two places laid, rather close together, for dinner. After a shower and hanging my washed clothes precariously out of the window I went to try and learn a bit about where I am staying. It wasn't easy as there are no notices on the walls or people around to talk to and it just seems a bit like a university hall with an Alpha feel to it. For a while I sat in a dark domed chapel, which I found behind a door on the ground floor, and listened to the organ being played by an old woman lit up on a balcony. I found a room of archives and many other doors I did not feel brave enough to open, each labelled with pilgrim destinations. Although I am in room number 308 I have not seen a single other person. My feet are far too sore to see the city so instead I lay on one of the two beds in my room and filled up on sugar from the vending machine.

When seven o'clock came I was looking forward to meeting my dinner companion. There was one light on over the two set places and I sat down wondering whether to make more of a space between them or even push it opposite me rather than stare at a completely empty refectory, but I left it for the mystery person to decide. A little old creature of a woman brought me some filthy brightly coloured set pâté. I thought perhaps I should wait, mainly for grace, but I was so hungry and tired I began. A weird man appeared. He was very jumpy and eventually sat down next to me a little further away than the place was set. He was rather too thin to be happy, aged about fifty-three and very suspicious. We sat facing the empty tables and chairs and, you know, I did not think he was going to say a word to me. I attempted, in French, to excuse myself for starting and to tell him that I don't speak very good French. He replied in English 'Well, I understand you'. I got excited that we could actually have a conversation but it turned out his English was worse than my French so, failing to have much of a conversation, we sat in rather intense silence.

I was beginning to enjoy being in France. I grew up in a quiet corner of South West Scotland and there are not many people around. When you do see someone they always want to stop and chat for a bit. You can go shopping in the local town and have the same conversation, almost always about the weather, with the newsagent, the chemist and the Asda checkout girl, but there is something polite and friendly in making conversation which inevitably adds to the enjoyment of whatever it is you are doing. I lived for a time in London and found myself being looked at in a peculiar way if I smiled at people on the street or said any more than hello or thank you when buying something in a shop. In France whenever you walk past someone they always say 'Bonjour' or at the very least nod their head in acknowledgment of your presence. Most of the day I rarely pass people but in a town it becomes the most social part of my day and I like it. I smile at everyone and everyone smiles back. When I arrive somewhere for the night there is no confusion. They get straight to the point, show me my room and agree a time for me to leave, but it is all done with unforced manners and a smile as if they really enjoy their job and are genuinely pleased to have me to stay.

Arras – Bapaume. July

The day I left the *maison diocésaine* in Arras is the last time I remember thinking I might actually make it to Rome. I stepped through the wooden door onto the pavement and, looking back at the Gothic building I had learnt little about, I let out an exclamation while my tummy did a somersault and I really believed I would get to Rome. Although I still continued to start every day with an upset tummy I was getting into the routine of moving on each day and felt much more relaxed and happy. At the end of the day the soles of my feet were always sore but by the morning they had recovered and this pattern was manageable. I had gone 204 kilometres since Canterbury and looking back it seems incomprehensible that I gave no conscious thought to the 1880 kilometres ahead of me. But I didn't.

Enjoying speaking French, I stopped in a graveyard to say hello to a man watering the flowers. He was full of enthusiasm and when I told him I was going to Bapaume he held me by the wrist and walked me back to the chalk[2] track between the field and the wall of the graveyard. Taking my stick from me he started drawing lines in the mud as he reeled off all the directions for the next twenty kilometres. He handed me back my stick and just in case it was too much to take in, which it undoubtedly was, he went through the directions all over again, this time with enthusiastic hands pointing all over the place. I had no doubt where I was going but he never asked so I just smiled and listened. As I headed off down the track he watched with pleasure. In the distance I could see a tractor pulling a plough across the field. As it neared the edge I was walking up, the door flung open and the man pointed with a firm steady arm straight on up the track. I waved with glee and he nodded his smiling head before pulling the door and turning to go back across the field. Brief moments like these when someone wants to join in my solitary journey, bring to it such warm joy.

I am crossing an area of France where the Nord-pas-de-Calais borders with Picardie and the now vast expanses of arable farming were once the battlefields of many wars, most significantly the First World War. What a contrast it is to walk with such freedom across land that so many fought and died on. I passed several sectioned off areas where row upon row of generic white gravestones whisper the

---

[2] Arras is built on chalk. This gave it a key advantage during WW1 when tunnels were buried under the town to hide troops and store supplies.

horrors of the number of young lives lost. I lay flat out amongst them on the fertile green grass thinking what a fortunate generation we were born into.

It seems my feet begin to really hurt at 20 kilometres, so after 26 kilometres to Bapaume I was hobbling but happy as it felt like a nice place. There was one main street with a buzz of people shopping. I have a room above a restaurant where dinner is included in the price. The tablecloths are a sure sign of four courses, and by now I was getting used to being watched, with suspicion, out of the corner of other diners' eyes. I went to the church in search of a stamp for my pilgrim passport. A tourist office or hotel stamp will do but, although harder to locate, the church stamp is always the most ornate.

A man was varnishing the doors and stepping over his resting ladder I entered the very dark church. No one was there so I went back out to the light and held my passport out to the handyman as I looked up at him with a questioning face. He pointed to a house on the other side of the cobbled street with an equally puzzled expression. I rang the doorbell and a short old woman opened the door and scurried back inside. I followed her in, shutting the door behind me. We stood, me towering over her, in a simple office hidden from the street by a net curtain. I was well practised in my introduction of who I was, what I was, and where I was going. This always brought the same aghast response, 'toute seule?' 'toute seule?' 'toute seule?', all alone, all alone, all alone. The fear people felt on my behalf, particularly the women, brought out a warmth and admiration that they could not hold back. She stretched up her arms to touch my face and her eyes sunk with apprehension for my journey. I got my passport stamped and said what a nice town this is. 'Non, est sale' she replied whilst scrunching up her face in a very firm unattractive way that old French women seem to be able to do. Holding the words in my head, I went to the tourist office to ask what it meant.

I also asked the bored woman in the tourist office if there was anything in particular that I should see. She told me about a painting in the Town Hall, which, if I could get permission, I really should see. The doors of the Town Hall were wide open and everyone in the rooms off the ground floor looked busy enough not to notice me, so I fled up the stairs in search of the great painting. Taking up most of the wall at one end of a large room was a grotesque picture commemorating the Battle of Bapaume 1871. I stood pretending to give a lecture to an empty room.

Bapaume – Péronne. July

Today for the first time the sun shone bright enough for me to put on my red sunglasses. I was happy and had genuinely got to grips with looking forward to moving on each day rather than feeling daunted by it. As I passed the village hall in Villiers-au-Flos, not even a fifth of the way through the day, a smiling busybody called after me. I turned round to go and say hello. I told her how happy I was that the sun was out and she said she had bought the sun for her village and that is why I had not seen it for the past nine days. Together with her friend they were cleaning the windows of the village hall. She offered me coffee and biscuits. In I went and sat in a brown plastic chair as they brewed the coffee and fed me biscuits. As I went to leave, one of them insisted I put the rest of the biscuits in my rucksack and the other handed me an envelope full of individually wrapped, chewy sweets. I went on my way and within a minute one of the women was by my side on a bicycle. I stopped and she got off to push her bike beside me. She had a bad leg so before long she was back on the bike. I said goodbye again and went to turn left but she insisted the route was straight on, so without wanting to argue I took her advice and continued straight ahead. My guidebook clearly said turn left but I hoped that perhaps this might be a shorter way to the next village. After an hour I came to a T-junction with a busy main road. I got out my road map and found that I had gone at least 5 kilometres in the wrong direction. I spent the rest of the day trying not to curse the kindly-intentioned woman as my soles ached and my right leg below the knee became like a dead weight of pain.

Stopping to eat yet another ham and cheese baguette I dug out a tubi-grip from my rucksack and pulled it over my right foot securing it round my shin. I wished there was not so far to go after lunch and I just hoped I was not doing any serious damage to my leg. The further I went the more sore it got and so my pace slowed, dragging out the day even more. As I walked along the pavement below the terraced houses in the village of Moislains I looked up at a woman taking washing off her line and said in despair 'Je suis très fatigué'. She held my unhappy gaze for a second and then said 'Café?' I beamed and climbing the steps up to the garden I followed her into her house. She patted the seat of a chair in the middle of her narrow kitchen and I sat down, exhausted. After a call of his name her husband appeared and pulling up a chair, he sat right next to me. He did not draw his alcoholic breath while his wife stroked my head at the same time as giving me coffee, biscuits, a creamy lemon yogurt and an apple. I had no choice but to eat it all as they watched intently. He really did yabber on and was adamant that I understood what he was saying. When I laughed and said I didn't understand he was not happy so I then had to pay attention and thoroughly agree with what he was saying. The things I made out were the importance of not getting in a car with a man, how dangerous it was that I was alone, why wasn't I married and where was I going to stay. There was a lot more but I was too overwhelmed by the smell of alcohol and the soft touch of his wife's hand stroking my tired head to actually take in what he was saying. I got up to leave and Madame, who just about came up to my chest, made a great effort to reach up and give me a big kiss on both cheeks. It was absolutely wonderful. I had been craving some human contact and this gave me such comfort. She then gestured to her husband who was still telling me something very serious, to open the gate. I shook his hand mid-sentence and, feeling revived, walked on to Péronne.

My right leg, below the knee all the way down the firm bone of the shin, is unbelievably painful. So sore I don't actually know how I made it to the garden shed I am staying in. I knocked on the door of the house with a plaque saying Presbytery and a black man answered. 'Pèlerin?' 'Oui' I said and he went inside leaving the door open. A white man then appeared in the door way and walked straight out across the yard to unlock a wooden door of what looked like a garden shed. Inside were two beds, he pointed round the corner and said 'toilette' and turned to leave. I stood at the door and mimed locking it in an attempt to ask for a key. He looked at me as if to say I really do not know why you are asking for a key, so I moved to let him go. My room for the night could hardly look less cosy. It is not helped by the fact that two of the four walls are almost entirely glass. With no curtains and a view of the street I certainly won't be sleeping in my pink satin nighty.

There was a large cardboard box in between the beds on the front of which was a label saying *pour Lourdes infirme*. Intrigued, I opened it up and what a treat it was to find several hand-knitted patchwork rugs. I made a comfy pillow and a much more snug bed before going to have a look round the town.

Péronne sits on a hill in Picardie at the confluence of the rivers Cologne and Somme. It is a town which has suffered greatly throughout history from the many wars that surrounded it. Nowadays it is a peaceful place and, despite the fact that during the battle of the Somme it was occupied by Germans and was bombed throughout the First World War, there are some impressive remains. In the ruins of the 13th century château, which now houses a museum of the Great War, I went round a temporary exhibition entitled *Phantoms and Nightmares* in which contemporary art attempted to rekindle the horrors of war through modern means. Installations, video clips and whispering voices from hidden speakers demanded a response to the re-enacted scenes of the Great War. It said more about the gaudiness of installation art and the contemporary desire to shock than the reality of war. By now my feet were giving in, even without the weight of my rucksack, so I sat outside a café in the main square eating a huge salad.

That night I slept better than I thought I would in the garden shed. Soon after I had been let into it, a rather camp, hunchbacked priest knocked on the door and in a high-pitched voice, invited me to breakfast at eight o'clock the following morning in the presbytery. I was ushered into a dank, dull dining-room, overcrowded with clutter.

Shortly after, hunched over it, he brought in a tray with a thermos of coffee and two very ordinary slices of brown toast. Grinning he placed the tray in front of me and, without even drawing open the faded velvet curtains, he left through a door on the other side of the square room. I stretched for the coffee and at the same time heard the turn of a key in the door. As I drank coffee and spread the toast with runny jam I listened to Father having the noisiest crap I have ever heard. It put me off eating but it made me laugh and laugh. I slid a ten-euro note under the corner of the tray and, incapable of facing him without a smirk, left without saying goodbye.

Péronne – Laon. July

It poured with rain and for six kilometres I trudged along a slippery disused railway track. Tunnelling through overhanging trees, the boggy path was one long cloud of mosquitoes. I tried to waft them away but the buggers bit and bit like crazy. Most of the time when I attempted to slap them as they landed on my skin I would also lose my footing on the slippery path to the great pain of my right shin and blistered toes. When I finally made it out of the trees onto a tarmac road I was seriously concerned about my right shin. The pain had spread down into the arch of my foot causing me to wince every time it bent at the ankle. Trying to avoid bending my ankle, I walked on with a limp, dragging my right leg along with me.

The Via Francigena crosses a part of Northern France which is very flat. The land is all arable farming, the fields are vast and the rural villages are few and far between. It is my choice not to follow the road. I like the pure peace on tracks between huge fields where there are no people, railway lines or roads. However, today I was worried. My leg was giving up on me and there was not a village in sight let alone another person. As much as I tried, the pain of my right leg was making it more and more difficult to put any weight on my foot at all. Suddenly, for the first time in eleven days, I met a man; he was walking towards me with a huge silky golden retriever. I stopped and waited for him to get closer. Pointing at my bandaged shin I asked if there was a bus or train near by. He told me the villages were small and there was nothing. We both headed on in opposite directions and I told myself that I would stop in the next village and ask for help, but right now I had no option but to carry on.

It was not long until the track I was following crossed a tarmac road. With a blind bend to the left and unable to run I decided to limp down the road and cross at a safer point. Just as I was about to go a camper-van came round the corner and my eyes met those of an elderly couple through the domed windscreen. As if they had read my thoughts, the brake light went on and they pulled two wheels onto the verge. I limped up the side to the open window and the woman asked where I was going. At that moment I decided to say 'Saint Quentin', the largest city in the region and I thought it was safer to get a lift to a city than name a quiet country village. Having got out a map she pinpointed Saint Quentin and leaning her arm out of the window motioned for me to let myself in the side door. I sat in their mobile bedroom with two very over-excited poodles as we drove on. It was noisy in the back of the camper-van, so we exchanged smiles rather than attempting to converse. Soon we were rattling along a motorway and unexpectedly they pulled over at the first turning off to the right we came to. I had thought we were off to Saint Quentin but their stopping was my cue to get out and there was very little else for me to do. I said thank you and waved them off up the motorway as I stood in the drizzle wondering what to do next. Helpfully I was right by a big road sign, which read *St Quentin 12km.* However this road was far too big to walk along. I was way off my guidebook route so I bent over my bag to get out the road map and as my bottom faced the traffic a black Mercedes saloon pulled off the busy road into the lane beside me. The tinted window went down and a smooth man asked if I wanted something to eat, at the same time as pretending to put food in his mouth. 'Non merci,' I said without smiling too much. 'English?' he asked. 'Yes,' I replied. 'Where are you going?' As he wasn't pointing in the that direction I said 'Saint Quentin'. 'Me going to Vermand,' and he pointed towards his windscreen. I took time looking in my bag and once he had driven off I pulled out the map and shading it under my hood I looked for where I was. The large-scale maps that I have are really hopeless when it comes to anything other than the network of main roads. I stood puzzled by what an earth I should do.

It was not long before the Mercedes drew up again, this time pointing towards the motorway. The window came down and, lowering his head to look at me, the man said 'I go Saint Quentin'. There was no time for me to answer before he was out of his car, walking round it and springing the boot open on the way. He beat his chest whilst saying 'I good man, I father, I grandfather'. Frightened, I stood repeating 'non merci', 'non merci', 'non merci', as he made his way closer to me. His arm stretched out and he bent down to pick up my bag. At that very moment the gold cross on a chain around his neck sparkled in a glimpse of sunshine and I found myself saying 'Oui, c'est ça va?' 'Oui, Oui, ça va, me good man.' He put my bag in the boot and I slid into the leather front seat, alarmed at what I was doing.

I adopted two tactics: sitting very upright with my legs close together in a totally undemonstrative and easy-going manner and talking the whole way so as to avoid an atmosphere building. Not that either of these two things would have really helped in a more unfortunate situation but, having got in his car, they were my only hope. Bruno drove me all the way to the railway station while continuously attempting to persuade me to come and have something to eat with him. I convinced him I had to catch the 13:50 train to Paris, giving us plenty of time to find the station but not enough time for lunch. When we arrived he offered me money but I refused, he then said he would buy me a picnic, I said no again. I did not want to be ungrateful so when he offered me his half empty packet of cigarettes I gladly accepted them. Three kisses later, Bruno was gone and I was on the train to Laon with a throbbing leg.

Laon

Laon is an attractive city whose heart and oldest part sits on top of a hill surrounding the Cathedral which looks down to the new city below and out over the plains of Picardie. I headed straight up the steep steps to the narrow paved streets, silent medieval houses and great architecture of the ancient city. The Cathedral with its five towers soaring high at one end of the isolated hill was a magnificent sight.

I booked into what looked a charming hotel for two nights *soirée étape* and headed straight for the chemist. A pharmacy in France is on a par with going to a GP in Britain, although possibly better as you do not have to go anywhere else to pick up your prescription. They seem to have many more drugs that are sold legally over the counter and the pharmacists, even if only in dress, give the impression they know exactly what they are talking about. I sat on a chair and wound up my trouser leg before pulling off my tubi-grip. There was absolutely nothing to see and compared to my left leg it didn't even look that swollen but when I placed the gentle woman's hand on my shin and pointed my foot forward and back she made a very concerned French noise and headed back to the cabinet of drugs behind the counter. She sold me a packet of the strongest ibuprophen capsules, a roll of Elastoplast bandage and a tube of anti-inflammatory tendon gel.

I sat in my room, with my foot up on a pillow, massaging my shin until dinner. The next morning my leg was even worse and I knew there was nothing I could do except rest it. I dragged it to go and look at the Cathedral in the pouring rain.

La Cathédrale de Notre-Dame was built from 1155 to 1235. It is vast and is regarded as one of the greatest examples of the new Gothic architecture of its time. Inside it is full of light, a result of its very high pointed arch ceiling and accentuated by the use of white stone. The main façade has intricate stone carvings sensitively restored and if you tip your head back and look up towards the high towers you see two stone oxen peering down from a precarious position with diffident expressions. Legend has it that they commemorate the oxen who pulled the carts full of material for the building of the Cathedral. In such a small city it is wonderful to be able to stand back and stare at the building without it being obscured by tourists.

Not wanting to go back to my room despite the rain, I sat under a dripping awning of a café drinking coffee and eating the bag of biscuits

I had bought from the baker next door. I got out my sketchbook and drew a view up the street of the remains of the oldest building in Laon. This passed enough time for the rain to stop and my tummy to rumble. Having bought a picnic from a delicatessen I went to sit on the damp city walls looking out across the plains of Picardie at an evil sky. I ate at great speed, relishing the drama of the oncoming raincloud. Then the rain fell and I headed back to my room which was musty with drying washing.

I long to be back on my journey but I am exhausted and my leg is so sore that I can barely put my own weight on it, let alone carry a rucksack. I lay on the bed with my self-bandaged foot propped up on a pillow listening to the rain out of the window. I decided to dig out my rosary and to pray for my feet. I fell fast asleep and woke with an urge to go to Mass. Reception told me that if I left now I could make it to the six o'clock Mass in the church at the bottom of the hill. I descended the 207 wet steps with as much speed as my foot allowed and caught the end of a baptism before the church filled with old people. For the next hour Mass was more like a distant conversation as I experienced an overwhelming humbling feeling of something, which is hard to explain.

A sense of God is the only real thing that has got inside me since my accident. I know now that my life is not in my own hands and my fate is beyond my control. I had always lived thinking that if things ever got too bad I could end my own life. The thing I never thought about was what I would do if my own life were about to end itself. When I lay in St Mary's Paddington operating theatre with panic around me I felt an inner calm and peace, which made me happier than I have ever been. I smiled and laughed at them all and even when I insisted they took off my bra from under the open-backed nighty they had put me in and give it to my uncle, no-one found it quite as funny as me. I remember a lot from that room: the tattooed girl banging my wrist with a stubby wooden stick to get my vein up so as to keep me in a deep sleep; the calm of the surgeon's voice as he gave orders to those around him; the bright patterns of the painted walls along the corridor between the operating theatre and the ward.

I even remember the sombre expression of the black man holding the doors open for my bed to be wheeled through. The image of my pale self lying lifeless on a bed in the ward will always be a haunting memory of my decision to live. I now bear the full weight of the gift of life which is not mine to end at will.

It was during this Mass that I was reminded that I was walking to Rome for God. I owed it to him to show that I have the determination to live the life he has given me and in return I needed the time to work out where it was I went wrong. It was now clear in my mind that I had to keep going for him and my future. I walked back up the long steep flight of steps back to the hotel and went through to dinner.

It is a long thin rectangular dining room. The tables have crisp white tablecloths and small lamps with dark green shades. The silver cutlery shimmers in the lighting and the room feels rather more like a railway carriage than a hotel. I have a table reserved for one. I am led up to the far end of the room and sit squeezed in a corner looking down at the couples and families scattered around the other half. I have tried to make friends with the people who work here but they have no time for me. As they wait hand and foot on everyone else, I am left to pinch the coffee at breakfast from the table that has just gone and now I have sat with an open menu for twenty minutes, the same set menu I had last night. The charm of the place wears off when one notices the sycophantic service given to people who have an air of money. After dinner I returned to my room and packed my rucksack ready to leave. That night as I laid my head on the pillow I knew I was continuing tomorrow.

Every day from Laon onwards I said my rosary at some point, praying for my legs and feet, knowing there was little else I could do, but believing that with this they would keep going. There was not one day ahead when they did not hurt. The soles hurt every single day and although my right leg got better it became my left foot which gave me the greatest pain of all. My rosary was a huge comfort and the time spent saying it was always the least painful of every day.

Laon - Martigny-Courpierre. July

Finding a place to stay was not always easy in France. There are so few villages en route and when one does reach one it is not always obvious whether there is a B&B. Today, reluctant to walk too far, I was heading to a village not marked in the guidebook and therefore I only had my large-scale map to contend with. Although on the road it was easy to follow the signs, I decided to go cross-country as it looked shorter.

I was so happy to be back in the countryside where people have time and a smile. Even the pain of my leg was diminished by regular doses of ibuprophen although it gave me a terrible upset tummy. There were many forks in the track I was on so I resorted to following my compass in a straight line through hedges, across fields and over streams. This was a game we used to play at home as children so I was very happy re-living it and much to my surprise I arrived exactly where I wanted. It was Sunday again and I had forgotten to stock up on food. Fortunately I passed an open boulangerie where I had a poor choice of canned food. Sausages in lentils with a baguette seemed the best option even with an upset tummy.

I am staying in the most charming rather too perfect gîte in Martigny-Courpierre. The lamps in my room are miniature birdcages with real nests inside, one of the doors is open and the wooden bird is pinned to the corner of the bedstead. Despite the fact that today I did less than half my usual distance, I am absolutely exhausted. So tired I could not bring myself to stand up in the shower and sat in the base hoping my energy would not continue to drain away forever. I slept all afternoon and straight on through the night.

Martigny-Courpierre - Berry-au-Bac. July

The following day, due to the pain of my soles, I had to pull over and stay the night in something that looked as if it had been deposited from the USA. It was a trucker's motel on the edge of a very busy road. There were 19 rooms along a wooden strip of cubicles, each with their lorry-sized designated parking spot. The rooms went from 1 to 20 avoiding number thirteen. I turned up as a woman was cleaning and seeing the strain in my face she happily gave me a room for the night. Thankfully I had wrapped up the left-overs from breakfast when Madame went to fetch her visitors book. I ate a small piece of bread, a slice of cheese, half a flat sugary pastry, a Ferrero Rocher and the three mints from the ashtray. I packed my bag and got into bed knowing there was no chance of my making it to Reims tomorrow but too tired to start searching for a town to stay in on the way.

I was asleep within minutes and didn't wake until my alarm went off at seven o'clock the next morning.

Berry-au-Bac - Hermonville. July

I had been out for sixteen hours but it did not seem to make me feel any less tired. I was determined to continue and set off to find the canal, which would allow me to avoid the main road. It was only when it turned a corner that I realised I was in fact following a river. I had come upon a group of gypsies who, as soon as I answered their question, I regretted telling that I was alone. My gold St Christopher dangling round my neck was hypnotizing them as I tried to pronounce the name of the canal. With a sudden fear I turned and walked at great speed back towards the main road. Safely back with the traffic it was not long before I crossed a bridge and found the canal. Disappointingly, walking along a canal for several hours is not as nice as I imagined. The track was tarmac, mind-numbingly straight and there were no boats to wave at. A few bicyclists passed but the time it took from spotting them in the distance to their drawing level just added to the boredom of the long straight path. I turned off it into slopes of champagne vines and up into woods full of mosquitoes. I was now into the rolling hills of Champagne-Ardenne, leaving the flat planes of Picardie behind me. The mosquito bites made my limbs swell up and gave off more heat than the sunshine. I was running out of energy and knew I must stop in the next village, Hermonville.

It was a clean tidy place at the bottom of a steep winding road. I went to the central square and into the grocery shop. The young man sitting behind the counter enjoyed looking at me while I asked for a place to stay. He got a mobile telephone out of his pocket and made a call. He then looked up and said 'Non.' I asked 'Un autre?' 'Très cher,' he replied. I needed to sleep whatever the price so I asked for the number. He wrote it down and told me it opens at two o'clock. I thanked him and walked back towards the pizzeria I had just passed.

I felt exhausted and barely able to eat the chicken salad in front of me, I went to the loo and splashed my face with cold water. The restaurant was empty apart from the couple running it and their friend who were sitting round a square table next to me drinking rosé and smoking cigarettes. Abba was playing and I thought of my brother Geordie who would be bobbing on his chair to the beat. I got talking to the owners and Madame (Lili) was determined to find me a cheaper place to stay. She made a telephone call and by her response I knew she was grumpy at the price they quoted. She hung up the telephone and looking straight at me said, 'you come stay with me'. That was it, I had no option but to wait for lunch time to finish, the pizzeria to close and her car to take us bumping at great speed down the back roads of Hermonville.

Lili has shoulder-length blonde hair, dark at the roots. Her face is furious with the effort of life but her eyes glisten with character and warmth. Everything is done with firm determination and great speed. She flung open the front door of a cluttered house and called out at the top of her husky voice two indistinguishable names. A huge Alsatian came bounding through the arch between the kitchen and the sitting room and a timid greyhound stood in its shadow. Lili knelt down on the floor and smothered them in kisses as their tails swished from side to side somehow avoiding the overflowing ashtrays on every side table. Following her upstairs she opened the door to an orange bedroom where I dumped my bag. Looking at me she asked 'Douche?' 'Oui merci' I replied and we crossed the landing into her shambolic bedroom, which had a bath in the corner. She held out the shower attachment and showed me how to run the water through it.

Following her back to the landing she handed me a towel. Shutting
the door behind me I got naked and stepped over the G-string into
the bath. There was a knock on the door and in she came handing
me a bar of soap and a flannel. She then pointed to cotton pads and
makeup remover on her dressing table and I was flattered she thought
I needed it. Out she went and on came the shower with a great gust. It
flipped out of my hand like an angry snake and landed upright in the
bath, spraying across the room. I sat down and washed awkwardly
then hurriedly I mopped the floor with my dry towel. It would have
been too obvious to wipe her filthy dressing table and mirror so I left
them covered in a splatter of water, hoping it would dry before she
noticed.

I got into the orange bed, which smelt so much of dog it might
as well have barked. The glasses on the side-table were a sure sign
Monsieur snores. Just before I fell fast asleep Lili came in and handed
me a piece of paper with 22:00 on it. She then stood at the end of the
bed miming eating. I smiled and thanked her, not fully believing she
really meant dinner at 10pm. I heard the car speed off up the street
and I slept until I was woken by a firm knock on my door at 10:30pm.

John-Luke, Lili's husband, popped his head round the door and
said 'dîner'. Pulling on a jumper and some tracksuit bottoms I went
to join what sounded like a party downstairs. Lili flung her arms out
and gave me a great big hug. I then kissed hello a beautiful young
couple, brown from their holiday in Corsica. The girl, Agathe, spoke
good English. With her help I could at last communicate with these
extraordinarily kind people. They were all worried about me and
having looked in the mirror I would admit I appeared frighteningly
exhausted but I reassured them I was in fact very happy. This made
them all laugh. Lili cooked delicious raw hamburgers with an egg on
top and as Agathe translated, we all sat and chatted round the table.
Once dinner was finished, I kissed them all goodnight and headed
back to bed.

Knowing I was safe and that these people wanted nothing other
than to be kind I lay amused by the thought that no one would ever
guess where I was. I had surrendered myself to others and gone

where the path led rather than plan the path to follow. The kindness of these people gave me confidence to trust others along the way and not judge them with a suspicious eye. I listened to my conscience and kept my wits about me but, by not judging others, I saw a wonderful side of human nature that came for free and in abundance and all I had to do was to give generously in smiles and manners on both the good days and the bad days. I was beginning to realise this journey was not about getting to Rome. Rome was where it would end if I got there but this reward would only come if I listened and learned on the way. There were many times ahead when I gave myself the option of going home and many, many days I lost belief in reaching Rome, but every night I packed my bag and every morning I walked on.

Hermonville - Reims. July

After breakfast with Lili in her dressing gown, one bosom popping in and out as she raised her arm to take short drags from her cigarette, she insisted on driving me to Reims. Off we took in her rattling car. As we pulled on to the motorway she grasped the steering wheel in two hands and announced 'Jaguar'. We careered into the centre of Reims at great speed. She refused to take any money, we hugged and kissed and I headed off to find a sports shop. I had worn through the tread of my trekking shoes and my socks no longer had backs to the heels. Having bought the most expensive walking boots as well as two fresh pairs of socks, I went to have a look at the Cathedral.

Like Laon la Cathédrale de Notre-Dame in Reims was another impressive 13th century Gothic building. The façade, which I approached from a long boulevard, is overwhelming in its delicate tracery. The three porches are adorned with skilfully sculpted figures and animals bringing the biblical scenes to life. Its craftsmanship is all-encompassing, a sight that once seen is engraved in one's memory as if the sculptor had somehow carved it out. Its reverence for God kept the fire burning inside me.

I found my way to another imposing *maison diocésaine* and was given a simple room. Reims is a crossroads for the hordes of people going to Santiago de Compostella and the sparse few heading down the Via Francigena to Rome, so I thought that I would certainly meet another pilgrim staying — but no, I was the only one. This did mean that after a good night's sleep I could eat almost a whole baguette at breakfast without feeling self-conscious. I put the rest up my sleeve and took it back to my room and into my bag for lunch. I was full of energy and looking forward to the day ahead.

Reims – Trépail. July

My boots were a joy. So much lighter and my toes had space to wiggle, however my right leg continued to hurt. It was such a dead weight that it felt as if I was actually carrying someone else's rather hopeless foot along. I left Reims along the boringly straight Canal de l'Aisne à la Marne but it was not long before I was climbing into hills of champagne vines, passing the iconic windmill of the Mumm & Co. Château. Despite the grey sky I was happy to be stumbling through prettier countryside and the tidy champagne villages of Verzenay, Verzy and Villiers-Marmery.

I had booked myself into a gîte in Trépail and I knew that when I reached the Forêt de la Montagne de Reims I was nearly there. The forest had no obvious tracks through it and every line of trees looked like a path both horizontal and diagonal. With my stopwatch set I followed the left and right directions in my book as accurately as possible. However, when I got to a line that read *turn right and proceed down the hill into the village of Trépail. Wooden training barns behind you* I could see neither a hill, nor a village, nor even what they meant by a training barn. I had been walking deeper into the wood for half an hour and I was now lost. At first I was so at ease with being lost that I set up my camera to take a photograph of myself pulling a caricature lost face. I then got out my compass and walked eastward hoping it would bring me to Trépail. I timed myself for half a kilometre and disappointingly I just seemed to get deeper into the damp, silent wood. I came upon a track which I was sure must lead to the village so, abandoning my compass, I followed it. When I came to an enormous uprooted tree I clambered over it to find no sign of the track on the other side. Time was passing and I was beginning to feel a little uneasy. It was very quiet in the forest and I was surprised because if there were a village as close as it should be surely I would hear something. I looked around but all I could see were trees, rows of them way into the distance. It was impossible to get any height to see anything and I definitely was not anywhere near the hill I supposedly had to go down. After an hour, covering a lot of ground, stumbling in a circle, I had no idea which direction I had come from and which direction to go in. Every tree looked the same and there were no markers, paths or signs anywhere. I decided to head in a straight line and just keep going and hope eventually I would come to a road before dark. I set off with the speed of a pounding heart when suddenly I heard the snap of a branch and turned around. Very close behind me was a large man in a bright red jumper and white trainers. The voices of all the people who have said 'c'est dangereux' rushed round my head and the thought 'This is the end' flashed through my mind. How and from where this man appeared I will never know but right then I knew I had to get out of the wood as soon as possible. Miraculously I heard a distant dog bark; it was coming from my left and I turned to head directly that way. The man stumbled, trying to keep up with me as I bounced my rucksack through the wood at great speed. I ground to halt, as ahead of me was an almost vertical drop of 20 metres I turned around and said 'Bonjour'. He looked more terrified than me. I did not understand a word he said but giving off an air of as much control as I could muster I decided he was lost too. I got my compass out and, knowing the village lay to the East of the wood, I wanted to see which direction we were heading in. The compass pointed East over the top of the edge we were standing on. While I stood still the fear was building back up inside me and in a split second I decided that, however much it might damage my right leg, I was going to go over the edge. I headed for the first trunk and from tree to tree I slipped all the way down to the bottom of the steep wet slope. I turned around and there was the man following my method of getting down. I called up 'Ça va?' 'Oui, oui,' he shouted back. There was a line of green bushes in front of me and as I looked at it I heard the reassuring bark of the dog, now much closer. I pushed through foliage and on the other side was a grill of brambles and a two-metre drop onto a tarmac road. I really would ruin my leg if I jumped down so instead I pushed back through the bush and waited for the man to follow. Down he slid onto the road and close behind him I put one hand on his shoulder and held one of his with my other and he lifted me safely down. We turned in opposite directions and thankfully I never saw him again.

Down the road I went into Trépail and asked a sweet-looking farmer in the village for the road with my gîte on it. 'Ici,' he pointed. I was standing with my back to the door and on it was a notice saying they had gone away on holiday. I looked at him with an amused but slightly desperate face. He pulled out his mobile telephone and made a call. 'Restez ici,' he said. Within five minutes a car pulled up, a woman got out, shook my hand and popped the boot. I put my bag in it and got into the front seat with no idea who she was or where we were going. She seemed trustworthy though rather aloof. We drove to the edge of the village where she parked and took me into her house. Having asked if I wanted to stay the night, she took me upstairs to a simple room in the attic. I put on another t-shirt and went downstairs. Lunch was still being mulled over by a table of friendly faces. I introduced myself with a huge smile and sat down in the one free chair. I pointed to myself saying 'Alice' then pointed at each of them. They went round the table giving me their names and place in the family. There were a husband and wife, friends of the family, a much elder husband of the woman who picked me up, their son and his wife. The woman who picked me up stood with her back to the counter smiling but it was a sad smile. The rest of them were full of the empty bottle of wine in the middle of the table and pushed the apple tart my way. It was delicious and once I had eaten two large slices and exhausted my French trying to explain what I was up to, I went back to my room to shower and sleep.

At seven o'clock I heard my name shouted up the stairs. In the kitchen there was a table laid for three. I sat down with the ancient husband who only had one working arm. The other was strapped closely to his chest having been bitten by a dog. He was a frail, thin man with an irritable expression and his wife now looked even unhappier than before and could hardly bring herself to smile. I presumed they had been arguing. After the old man I helped myself to tomatoes, lettuce and bread. Just as the woman was pulling her chair out to sit down the doorbell rang and she went round the corner to answer it. The old man started eating so, taking his lead, I began too. At first I tried to make conversation but I soon gave up because the simpler my questions got the more he made out he could not understand me. He kept getting up from the table. At first it was to turn the oven off. Then he went to turn it back on again and fried two burgers with one arm. Refusing any help he also managed to get one burger out of the pan, onto a plate, cut in half and pushed under my nose for me to accept if it was cooked enough. Meanwhile Madame was still round the corner in deep conversation with another woman. The old man tried to tip the other burger out of the pan onto my plate but I stopped him. I was now the only person sitting at the table and therefore the only one eating. The spare burger went in the bin and the man left the room. All three people then reappeared. I shared a very firm handshake with someone who turned out to be Madame's sister. They were two of the unhappiest people I had seen. Neither of them smiled and their faces held a look of concern. Some cheese was put on the table and I tucked into it while they all headed back into the hall. Finally Madame came back and sat at the table. She offered me apple tart, which I accepted thinking I would keep her company while she ate. She didn't eat a thing and sat in silence with a mind far away. Looking up at her I saw she was crying so I got up and put my arm round her shoulder. Through slow tears she told me her father had a very bad heart. He was 83 and in hospital. She then stood up and left the room. I cleared the table and whilst filling the sink the old man appeared and barked something at me, which clearly meant do not wash up. I went to bed amazed that in the circumstances these people had given me so much but also looking forward to getting out of there tomorrow.

Trépail - Châlons-en-Champagne. July

After descending the Montagnes de Reims, not that they qualify as mountains, I followed the Canal Lateral à la Marne all the way to Châlons-en-Champagne. Canals really are deadly to walk along but the good thing is it has put me off wanting to go on a barge holiday. The water is filthy and I would be longing to swim in it and although everyone on the infrequent boats waved with a happy smile, I did wonder what they do all day other than move at a very slow pace up an incredibly straight bit of water.

Châlons-en-Champagne is situated at the crossroads of the river Marne and a Roman road, the Via Agrippa, that linked Rome to Boulogne-sur-Mer. As a commercial centre the city grew in wealth and population, hence the impressive architecture and grand squares. Today it is a provincial city surrounded by vast chalky plains of arable land. On the way in I visited La Cathédrale Saint-Étienne. At first this cathedral looks like a monstrosity but, once inside, the culmination of the styles, spanning the twelfth to the seventeenth century, create a sacred space hidden within the city, which has declined.

I went to the tourist office in search of somewhere to stay and picked up several leaflets telling me about the city which is full of art, yet at the same time I get the sense that it is a rough place. There seem to be no tourists despite plenty to see and instead the streets are full of Goths on BMXs. Both the bank and the glass-fronted shopping centre are manned by heavy-booted security guards, adding to the uncivilised air. I got directions to a hotel and headed off through the streets of half-timber houses, looking forward to the clean sheets and array of bathroom products.

As always in hotels, the woman at reception looked at me in such an unwelcoming way that it made me feel way beneath her. Universally hotel receptionists give me the impression they would really rather not have a weary traveller for the night despite the fact I pay the same as everyone else. Apart from a trip to the supermarket to buy dinner I remained in my room, taking full advantage of the luxury and comfort and lounging around with no clothes on.

Châlons-en-Champagne - Coole. July

I had breakfast in a café before leaving Châlons-en-Champagne. I sat at a table outside, drinking coffee and eating a pain au chocolat, as the street sweeper rested and the children crossed the square to school. There was so much I had not seen here but my feet were far happier having rested for so long. I bought food on the way out of town knowing I was heading into exposed countryside.

Today I bored myself into hysterical outbursts walking along a straight, bright white chalk Roman road. I walked for twenty-seven kilometres looking into and back at the same view. It stretched for kilometre beyond kilometre as far as I could see, like a big thick stripe of white tempera, rolling up and down small rises as the huge plains of farmland stretch out on either side. I had not seen a single person close by or in the distance all day so when I arrived in Coole where I hoped to stay the night I was longing for some human contact. Through my experiences so far in France I had learnt that Town Mayors are self-important and a little bit of flattery could get me a long way. So when I quickly realised Coole was too small to even support a shop I headed for the town hall in the hopes of winning over the Mayor. The door was open but no one was about so I climbed up the stairs to have a further look and found myself in some other family's home. The husband kindly walked me down the street to the farmhouse of the Mayor, Monika Songy, and her husband, Jean-Pierre. The Songys' farm comprised most of the other buildings in the village and the Via Francigina pilgrim sticker on their front door made me hopeful they would give me a bed. Unlike most other countries, French farmhouses are incorporated into the village and the fields lie around the outside. In contrast, it is far more social than the lonely crofts in quiet Scottish valleys or the huge farms of Australia and New Zealand.

From the moment I walked through the Songys' door it was as if I were their own daughter. Monika hugged me hello and took me upstairs to a large double bedroom. It was their son's who had now left home and the only evidence of a child was the wallpaper patterned with a repetition print of racing cars. I was then given a tour of the house, two more bedrooms, one of which was hers and her husband's, a room for drying clothes (which would be a garage if cars could drive upstairs), the office, the sitting room, the kitchen and the fridge. Monika, who speaks fairly good English, hardly drew breath and whenever a new conversation started we stood still so my poor feet had a long time to wait before I could finally sit down.

Having showered I headed back downstairs to pick up the conversation where we left off. Jean-Pierre had appeared and with a shy smile and dipped eyes he shook my hand and called for Monika. She came into the kitchen with a large selection box of tea. With great excitement she chose 'English Breakfast'. I boiled the kettle and filled a pot and we sat round the table drinking black tea as Monika overflowed with enthusiastic chatter. She wanted to know everything about my home and my family and insisted that while I was here I treated it like my house. I then said I would help her in anything that needed doing so we went to dig new potatoes and pick French beans from the vegetable garden. As we crossed the yard it filled with inquisitive people from all corners. I was introduced to her brother-in-law, her very old parents-in-law, her son and his girlfriend. I kissed them all hello and stood smiling while Monika repeated to them everything she had learnt about me so far. They all watched her intently, occasionally glancing to smile at me.

Back inside I said I was going to go to sleep and they both looked at me with surprise. I explained that I had a bad head and needed to sleep a lot. They said I would have a peaceful time as they were going to a wedding at four o'clock and then on to a party so would not be back until late. I was amazed that they would entrust their house to a complete stranger. Before I went upstairs Monika gave me five large photograph albums of their group holidays with the few other people in the village. These were very entertaining more for the fact she thought I would be interested to see their trips to Africa, America and India. I suppose if I were family, which is how she was treating me, then of course I would want to see the photograph albums.

Having slept most of the afternoon I took advantage of being able to use the washing machine and dressed in a long t-shirt from the laundry room I washed everything in my bag and fortunately found a tumble dryer under the stairs. Meanwhile I folded all their laundry in the drying room and made a delicious salad from fresh vegetables in the fridge and new potatoes we had dug up that afternoon. It was such a great feeling to be alone but in a home. I wished I had something to give them but they even refused money. Not only did I get a great night's sleep but also Monika had telephoned the Mayor in the next village and arranged for me to spend a night in the village hall. I set off with no worries and a bag full of clean clothes.

Coole - Corbeil. July

I rejoined the Roman road and walked in a very straight line for twenty kilometres. The sun shone bright, there was no shade, and by the time I reached Corbeil Village Hall I was dehydrated and exhausted. The key was under the mat and I unlocked the door to a stone floor and an empty room. There was a loo round the corner but nothing soft in sight. Despite sore feet and a heavy head I thought I would go and introduce myself to the Mayor and just hope perhaps she would give me some food at the very least.

Madame and Monsieur Mirofle were both at home clearing away lunch and they could not have been more full of smiles. They didn't speak a word of English or understand my French but with much confusion it turned into one of the most memorable nights.

Their house, set back from the road, was festooned with hanging baskets full of brightly coloured flowers. The front door was open and Monsieur stood smiling at me as I crunched my way across their gravel yard. I was welcomed straight into the kitchen and, sat on a chair pulled into the table, I was given a glass of water.

Madame and Monsieur Mirofle were very short, humble people. Her face held a look of angst but through it came a timid smile. She had short wavy grey hair, and stood with her legs awkwardly apart which made her hips seem unusually wide. Monsieur Mirofle, only slightly taller than his wife, had a domed bald head and, above his ears, very tidy patches of hair that only just met at the back of his head. His jeans were so clean that they barely crumpled when he walked. He moved without energy but with an unimposing calm and peacefulness. They were sweet to each other in a non-tactile way and waited on me in quite a subservient manner.

After I had drunk two glasses of water and slipped into the silence of their company they asked if I wanted to have a shower. I was so pleased and, standing in a narrow corridor, I dug a change of clothes and a towel out of my rucksack. Madame insisted I used a clean towel and handed me one together with a hand towel and a flannel. When I came out of the bathroom there on the other side of the door were a pair of slippers. My feet sank into the comfort of them and I entered the kitchen with a big smile on my face. Madame showed me into a room next to the kitchen, with a sofa, and said 'reposez'. I told her I needed to sleep and that I would go back to the Mairie. As they stood very close together staring at me her husband said something to her and in return she said to me 'Vous voudrez un lit?' I tried to say I would love a bed but if it were difficult I would go to the Mairie. They simply did not understand and looked at me almost crossly, so nodding my head I said 'oui'.

I slept until six o'clock on a soft sprung, clean, double bed in a room decorated with miniature figurines and wide-eyed china dolls. When I woke I wasn't quite sure what to do but headed downstairs. No one was in the kitchen so I went out into the yard and across to a large wooden barn. Inside I found Monsieur labelling jars of clear honey. I watched for a bit and then headed back into the house where I found Madame laying the table and watching the TV at the same time. Thank goodness for the TV as despite the table not facing it, it gave us all something to crane our necks at and fill the silence during dinner. It is so frustrating not speaking French but it makes it particularly difficult in a place where the people don't talk. Their life is so simple, immaculate and perfect that humour has no part in it. They live in a humble world where the flowers blossom, the bees produce honey, and a bottle of wine lasts a week.

As I pushed my chair back from the table, a screech broke the still silence, and I moved to get up. We agreed breakfast at 7:30 and after that I could not work out what they were trying to say. They were both either telling me or asking me something. They would speak and then just smile for so long that it became obvious they expected more than just a smile in return. They said 'oui' still smiling so I smiled even more and repeated 'oui' back. They then looked at each other and nodded more times, turning back to me with a less questioning smile. I knew the plan had been made but had no idea what I had agreed to.

Corbeil - Brienne le Château. August

After a long sleep I was back downstairs for breakfast. Madame looked so cosy wrapped up in a bundle of fluffy dressing gown. She served me coffee as I modestly tried not to eat too much of their baguette. Breakfast didn't last long and afterwards she wrapped up a sausage roll and handed it to me with a carton of fruit juice. I put it in my bag and kissed her goodbye, regretting I could not express how grateful I was. Outside Monsieur was attaching a trailer of beehives to a white Citroen van. As I walked towards him he opened the passenger door as if for me to get in. I got in and, remembering our Babel-like pact last night, I was not going to attempt to ask any questions.

We must have driven for half an hour, in silence, as slowly the beehives were pulled gently down the Roman road. Turning off it we headed through a village and down a bumpier track towards a wood. There was nothing threatening about this man so I was quite happy looking out of the window despite not knowing what was going on. After a real struggle reversing the trailer into an opening in the wood we both got out of the car. He began to detach the trailer while I stood watching. He pointed at the hives and said 'abeilles'. I repeated it in my head as 'abees' and continued to do so for many more days. Copying exactly what he did, I got back into the van. We then headed back down the track and into the village where he pulled over in the main square. Pointing his arm in front of me and stretching towards the side window he said, 'tout droit, tout droit, tout droit'. I kissed him four times and set off to rejoin the Roman road, the view of which was now driving me mad.

26 kilometres later, I was in Brienne-le-Château and my days on the Roman Road were over. I am staying in a cell. It is my third free night in a row and having got the key and a map from the tourist office I found my way to this depressing pilgrim hostel. It consists of three old hospital beds in a concrete room. Little light comes in from the one window which has thick metal bars on the outside. After a hunt for the fuse box I turned on a dull overhead light and read the visitors book, which cheers the place up a bit although the small number of pilgrims suggests I will be alone.

Brienne-le-Château is an odd place. I was sitting on a bench eating an ice cream and the first person to hobble past was an old man who stood staring at me whilst saliva dripped from his lips. When I looked up to smile at him he seemed to take it as a threat and walked off. Shortly after another elderly man approached me and started shouting at me in French. At first I found it quite funny but this made him even more cross and clenching his fist, he raised his arm and shook it in front of his face with great force. Since the bench was in an open square with plenty of people around I was not afraid but thought it best to move on. As I got up, the man, no longer interested in me, sat in my place.

I headed to the supermarket to buy dinner and in the confectionery aisle I saw a sweaty man weighed down with a rucksack pushing two walking poles in his empty trolley. The slogan on the front of his t-shirt read *Help for Heroes*. I said 'You must be English'. 'Yes,' he smiled shaking my hand, 'I'm Andrew Bruce'. He stood rocking on his boots, flicking his rucksack straps as if they were braces saying 'I've walked all the way from London and I'm going to Rome.' Then turning to a blond woman who had sprung up by his side, he said 'meet my friend Vanessa Fox'.

Vanessa, who is Canadian, got her iphone out and took a picture of Andrew and me standing in the aisle. After twenty-one days alone and now meeting two English-speaking pilgrims I had to try hard not to cry. I told them I was also hoping to walk to Rome and asked if they were staying here but much to my disappointment they said they didn't like the look of the outside of the pilgrim accommodation so they were hoping to find a hotel in the next town. Agreeing with them I said 'The town has a peculiar feel to it' and they told me the château is a psychiatric hospital. I said goodbye and Andrew gave me his mobile number, saying I could call whenever I needed help or company. As I turned to go he said 'Make sure you lock yourself in tonight, that place doesn't look too safe'. I cheered myself up walking back through the town pretending I was on the set of *One Flew Over the Cuckoo's Nest.*

Brienne le Château - Bar-sur-Aube. *August*

Spending most of the day outside, the elements in direct contact with your skin, eating under an open sky and going to the loo behind bushes, makes the shower, the scent of soap, the warmth of the water and lying on a bed naked to dry off at the end of the day pure pleasure.

I had arrived in Bar-sur-Aube having spent most of today alongside the banks of the river Aube, a huge relief after the last seventy-three kilometres almost entirely on the straight Roman road. As I turned the corner to go into a longed-for hotel I heard my name shouted up the street. There was a waving arm, like a windmill cutting the horizon, and Andrew Bruce with an enthusiastic rush of energy came bounding towards me. He kissed me on both dehydrated cheeks and went full speed into conversation. I was too exhausted to take it in. Despite all staying in the same hotel it was two days until I saw Andrew and Vanessa again. In the meantime I met two wonderful nuns.

Bar-sur-Aube - Clairvaux. *August*

Having left Bar-sur-Aube after a much needed good night's sleep I entered the Clairvaux forest, paying close attention to my stop-watch and compass, determined not to get lost. I reached Clairvaux in good time and when I arrived I thoughtlessly pottered through the gates of the old Cistercian Abbey, now a high security prison for life offenders, to see if I could have a look round. Inside the walls the atmosphere was strangely hostile. The information office was closed and I headed up to the main door of the prison. Intimidating, muscular men with large guns on their belts guarded it. As they stared at me I decided I did not like the feel of the place at all and turning around I headed straight back out of the gates. It was absolutely pouring with rain but not one bit of me wanted to stay in this town. I sheltered in a bar and rang Muma to see if she could search for any accommodation near by. She texted me back with the address for the Fraternity of St Bernard, which was the only place she could find at all close to where I was. The Fraternity was in the town and I reluctantly made my way to it. There was no answer when I rang the bell and as it was tipping with rain I decided to try the door. It opened and I let myself in to a cosy room of motley furniture.

Then the door flung open and, cowering from the rain, an elderly nun entered. I leapt up and introduced myself. She could hardly get her words out she was smiling so much. I was greeted with two kisses and shown to a simple room upstairs. This place was a pocket of warmth in a cold street. Having slept for four hours I went downstairs and into a kitchen full of people from the village. They were eating brownies baked by one of the younger girls and when they pushed the tin my way I gladly accepted. Conversation was difficult but smiling, laughing and talking back in English made it all great fun for them and me. There was such excitement when the filthy crème anglais came out of the fridge but much to their disappointment I just could not bring myself to have any. When they all stood up and made signs of praying I followed them through the house and we crammed into a cupboard disguised as a chapel. Sharing a book with the man next to me, across our touching thighs, we all sang something for half an hour.

The village people left and I joined four German bicyclists, the two nuns, one of their sisters and her 93-year-old friend on a long table for dinner. It was such good fun and I thoroughly enjoyed telling elaborate stories in bad French with self-conscious acting, to the complete pleasure of the old women up my end of the table. I had noticed there was only one set of cutlery so, with a rumbling tummy, I piled the ravioli on to my plate. It turned out there were in fact four courses and I ended up eating so much I had to go to bed before the washing up.

The bicyclists were two sets of married couples following the St James's Way over the course of four years. They were nice but devoid of charm and warmth, not helped by the harsh cold tone of their accent whether speaking German or English. As I ploughed my way through a bowlful of ravioli the Germans seemed rather more health-conscious in their approach to dinner. The women barely ate a thing and whereas when I finished the water jug I swung back on my chair, they were clinical in their table manners and the tightness of their skin over angular bodies made even a smile look harsh. As one of the nuns spoke good German they made little effort to move away from conversation up her end of the table. However in time I talked to them about two things.

Firstly they could not get over the fact I didn't use a GPS to follow the route. Despite being on a road they had two GPSs, however they seemed to disagree about whose was better. To me a GPS takes away the charm of a journey. If you know exactly where you are going, you stop paying attention to the getting there and consequently miss out on what is going on around you. Also by getting lost you inevitably get to know the area a lot better than you would otherwise, which I see as an unintentional advantage.

They said it would be much quicker if I rode a bike to Rome, so I told them I'd had a bad accident on a bicycle and preferred to walk. They asked about the accident in an analytical way which, when language is a barrier, makes for a pretty unpleasant conversation. Nothing was left to the imagination and, regardless of feeling, they wanted to know every detail. These pilgrims were certainly not the type I dreamed of meeting.

Almost the best part of staying with the nuns was the amount of kisses they gave me. It seemed that every time I re-entered the room it gave them an excuse to give me another kiss. It was slightly unusual but so comforting. At breakfast they both appeared with a pair of woollen socks for me. I was so touched because at dinner I had joked that the countryside is beautiful but it is very difficult to find a sock shop amongst the vines. I left with a warm feeling inside me having come across two affectionate and fun-loving nuns in a town better known for life sentences.

Clairvaux - Richebourg. August

The following night I shared a cottage in Richebourg with Andrew and Vanessa. Independently we had both ended up pleading with the same farmer's wife for a place to stay and she had let us rest in her empty holiday cottage for one night. I had arrived before them and was ready for bed, despite the fact it was only 4pm, by the time they and their walking poles came crashing through the door. We sat round the kitchen table for a while getting to know each other. Andrew comes from Dumfries-shire, the next door county to me in Scotland and being British and of a certain class he soon started reeling off names of people we might know in common. As he sat with his top off and bare unchiselled chest opposite me, he told me the staggering amount of money he had raised for *Help for Heroes* and that he hoped to arrive in Rome a week before his 50th birthday.

While Andrew showered I spoke to Vanessa who I think is his girlfriend although she lives in Canada and he lives in London, but they are sharing a double bed and walking together for at least a month. Either way I admire the fact they can do both and still be so unbelievably cheery. They met a year ago walking the Northern Route of the Camino de Santiago. I asked her why she came to Europe to walk and she touched the table and said in her drawn out accent, with complete sincerity and a wide open mouth; 'You know this may be real or it may not, you know what I'm saying Alice'. I nodded in disagreement. 'I hope to see something, like a vision or something out of this world, I haven't seen it yet so that's why I keep comin'.'

Richebourg - Langres. August

Having got up earlier, it was not until they walked past me the next morning that I saw Andrew and Vanessa again. They moved at a much quicker pace than me and the distance between us grew. I flung back my head, stuck out my tongue for the drizzle, watched the deer in the hay fields, attempted to keep up with the butterflies and happily paced along to Langres. I soon found out that Andrew and Vanessa followed the main road and because I tended to avoid the road as much as possible we saw little of each other during the day. To begin with I could not work out if I missed them or not but soon the distance between us grew days apart and walking with them was no longer an option.

The fortified town of Langres is on top of a steep hill and the walls and city gates, still intact today, make an imposing entrance which, just to walk through, gives one a sense of achievement. On my search for a bed I had a look inside the Cathédrale de Saint-Mammes which lacked the light and grace of later Gothic buildings and consequently it appeared gloomy inside. I came out and asked a man on the street where the tourist office was. He gave me directions to the other end of town and sent me with a message to say 'bonjour' to his son who works there. On my way I went into a delicatessen and, making friends with the shopkeeper, I asked if I could taste the local cheese, which takes its name from the town. He happily cut me a quarter of one of the smaller cylindrical cheeses and I stood eating it as he eagerly waited for my reaction. It was slightly dry in contrast to its soft creamy colour but very tasty and with my limited French I gave him an expression to say that was delicious. We smiled at each other as, having left, I passed his window on my way down the street.

I find it easy to make friends with old people but women, particularly young women in towns, are harder work. I had to pay the woman in the tourist office one euro to call the hotel she recommended and find out if there was room before I trudged there on very sore feet. Having been dismayed at the lack of welcome from her I then got an even frostier welcome from the girl at the hotel reception. I often take things far too personally and feel unnecessarily hurt by people. This girl at reception really knocked my confidence, as I was too tired to take her charmless manner. Having asked if there was Internet, she handed me a lengthy code. I stood typing it into my telephone only to get a message saying *password invalid.* I then struggled to ask in French if the password included spaces and capital letters or not. She was absolutely no help and stood staring at me, eyebrows raised, pulling a face, which said you are the most stupid girl and I really don't understand what on earth you are trying to say. In need of a shower, with my backpack on and my stick dangling from my arm as I struggled to hold my telephone with both hands, I looked up at her and said, 'I guess it isn't going to work then,' and turned to go upstairs. 'It does work,' she said. Astounded, I turned around and exclaimed, 'you speak English?' 'Yes,' she barked as if to say 'Why wouldn't I?' We then of course easily got the Internet working.

I went to my room with the length of the day catching up on me. Longing to be lying in bed I showered and too tired to stand I leant both elbows on the glass shelf above the sink, propping up my chin on them to look at my weathered face in the mirror. The brackets gave way and as if in slow motion the shelf dropped, sliding off the sink and shattering all over the floor into thousands of aquamarine pieces. My feet were grazed enough to bleed and I struggled without gloves to gather up all the tiny shards, leaving no evidence except in the bin. I collapsed on the bed, feet throbbing, and cried and cried.

I lay with deep uneven breaths in my chest and wet eyes staring at the ceiling, wondering what an earth I was doing walking to Rome. I spend the days thinking about how I am going to embark on a better, more fulfilling life, but I am struggling to find any answers. I really hoped that by creating a totally isolated circumstance I would have time to get to know myself and work out who I am and what my path in life is. I am concerned that it may be too late to embark on a new path and I worry how I would do it with dedication while at the same time wanting to get married, have children and secure a non-lonely life for the future. In the insecurity of struggling to feel or find any answers I am left wondering if there really is any more to this journey than the walking. I search, I think, I try so hard but tonight I am not sure I am getting any closer.

Langres – Les Archots. August

I woke at 5:30am with a churning tummy and spent at least half an hour on the loo. By nine o'clock I was feeling a little better and dragged myself up, unsure how far I would be able to go today. My rucksack felt heavy, my head was saying I want to sleep, and I was walking with not enough attention on the road. Had I not stepped on to the verge in order to jump across a hole in an attempt to put a spring in my step, a motorcyclist hugging the curb bent over like a monkey clinging to its mother, going too fast to move a millimeter, would have careered straight into me, and the poor woman driving the red Renault Clio would have been first on the scene. At times life really does come down to good or bad timing.

I entered Le Pailly, a small village with an inviting little church. I have seen several magnificent cathedrals but they lack something that some small village churches have in abundance. Inside, this church felt as though it had a warm fireplace at one end. The altar was lit with a clean, bright white light and the rest of the space receded into darkness except for the crack of light stretching in through the open door. There were carved wooden saints guarding the walls and empty pews down either side of a narrow isle. I liked it in here. Propping up my bag against a pillar, I sat near the front saying my rosary. Bent forward I could not stop the unhappy tears flowing from my eyes. My head just does not work like it used to and I no longer have all that energy I took for granted. In despair I thought about the reality of never being able to stay up late or get through a day having had a bad night's sleep. I heard a noise at my side and turned to see a woman at head height with me. 'Bonjour' I muffled and she asked if I was a pilgrim. The tears just would not stop, they flooded out of my eyes as I excused myself and said 'Oui. Je suis un pèlerin'.

Her gigantic round glasses magnified her eyes, which stared at me wide open, but her face remained expressionless. She offered me food and to begin with I said just coffee would be great but still wiping my tears and following her out of the dim church she said, 'Déjeuner à midi.' We walked to her house and she, Georgetta, talked a lot, some of which I understood but most I didn't. Though I longed to remove my boots and socks she said I could keep them on as we entered her small house. I sat at the table watching her cook. She wanted no help and just let me be in silence. There was a noise next door and in came her 'petit fils' Ewan who was black. Laying the table for four they chatted, as I remained inconspicuous in the corner. Georgetta must have been 65+ and Ewan perhaps early 20s. The front door opened and in came her sister-in-law Marie, who had come to visit from Paris. She was bright-faced and had immaculately painted toenails.

We had a four-course lunch of salami & salad, chicken legs and vegetables, cheese then fruit salad and finally a cup of coffee. We talked a bit together but, content just having me round their table, they let me drift in and out of fatigue and concentration. Giorgetta cleared and served everything, all done with frozen wide staring eyes and expressionless face. Maria took particular interest in the handle of my stick, which I found myself saying came from a black-faced sheep while staring at Ewan, then desperately hoping they understood every word I said. After lunch Georgetta and her grandson had a confrontational conversation, he left and Maria and Georgetta debated whatever the issue was as I sat not understanding a word. I then found myself helping Georgetta hang the washing on the line despite the drizzle. She went through each item 'moi', 'Ewan', 'moi', 'Ewan', 'Ewan', 'Ewan', as I pegged them; knickers, boxers, vests, socks and t-shirts, no one article causing any more shyness than another. Too short to reach the line other than on tiptoe, she was grateful for my help.

By now I was used to giving in to the will of others, which almost always led to a pleasant surprise. Georgetta picked up her handbag and I knew we were off somewhere. I kissed Maria goodbye since she was still sitting at the table and it appeared she wasn't coming. I followed after Georgetta, picking up my rucksack as we went out of the door. She opened up the boot of her silver Citroen and I put my bag in. Just as I was squeezing into the passenger seat she said 'Arrêt' followed by something I didn't catch. Round she came to my side of the car, pushed a rusty bicycle out of the way and motioned for me to follow her through a gap in the wall. In we went to another half of the garage where she removed a worn white sheet to reveal what looked like an old fashioned pram converted into some kind of wind instrument. From a box she unfolded a strip of cardboard with tiny rectangular holes all along it. Then feeding this strip into one end of the instrument she turned a huge handle and, as her bosoms ebbed on each revolution like the tide on a rocky shore, the most charming childhood tune filled the garage. I smiled and smiled as she turned and turned and the notes danced through the air. The cardboard grew through the machine like a big flat bit of spaghetti and the tune came to an end. Now we could get into the car.

She drove like many old women with bad eyesight; gears grinding, following a wiggly course on a straight road. Past a gîte that I noted for the night and on we went. Turning right down a track into the forest, on and on we bumped until we arrived at a church deep in the woods. It was dark inside with only a slight bit of light shining through the thick, deep coloured, stained glass windows. We crept up to a man and woman with their rosaries out. Georgetta kissed them both and I shook their hands—well, what remained of his, he having lost three fingers and been left with just a pinkie and a thumb. We all sat down in a row and for the next half an hour, in turn, they said a similar series of prayers. I sat peacefully not able to shut my eyes for fear of falling asleep. Just as I thought we were going to the car Georgetta led me into the woods and down to a grotto. Her little leather buckled shoes and short legs made for a very slow walk.

Back at the car I asked to go to the gîte and tried to explain that I was very tired. She drove me right to the door, we kissed goodbye and I wished I spoke enough French to thank her properly. In I went as she hovered outside, only leaving once I had waved goodbye from the window signaling that everything was O.K.

Les Archots - Champlitte. August

Much to the owner's surprise I slept from 4pm through an almighty thunderstorm and woke the next morning with restored energy and great inner happiness. I sat at an empty table laid for sixteen and wished I had had the stamina to stay up for dinner last night. I piled homemade strawberry jam onto a baguette so fresh it was as if it were savory candy floss. The day's walking was as easy as the breeze, light and effortless, through fields that had gone astray and were full of delicate wild flowers varying in colour depending on their length. I had crossed the large region of Champagne-Ardenne and was now into Franche-Comté, the last of four French regions before Switzerland. It was as if my feet were eating the kilometres and for a first time in a long time I got to the small town of Champlitte without too much pain.

I joined Andrew and Vanessa on a road shortly before the town and we all booked into the same hotel. I am in a saucily decorated room in a turret. There is a purple drape above the cushion-covered red square bed, a large mirror on the wall opposite, thin purple curtains hanging over the window and a fluffy deep purple rug on the floor. My room overlooks the roof of the kitchen and I am lying in bed listening to the sizzle of the pan and French chefs singing along to English Rock and Roll songs. Moments like this are too good not to share.

I lay in bed planning the next few days to Besançon and the end of the first of three guidebooks to Rome. This thought is so exciting I am going to celebrate with a day off.

Champlitte - Gy. August

It only took me two days to reach Besançon. I planned to spend a night in Dampierre-sur-Salon; however, it was such an empty depressing place with a dirty feel to it that I bought a delicious snail-shaped pastry and kept walking. I saw a sign in the next village for a B&B and headed where it pointed. Three children rushed out of the house as I walked through the gate with a B&B sign hanging at an angle on it. Having asked for a bed I do not know what they replied but it was clear there was no bed. I turned around regretting not stopping at Dampierre-sur-Salon or taking the road route via Grey with Andrew and Vanessa and went back to the trucker cafe I had just passed on the side of the road. I sat up at the bar on a high stool. The owner shook my hand as I ordered a cup of coffee. I tried talking to him and he called over the waitress who said in a friendly French accent, 'What do you want?' I told her I had a problem and that I needed somewhere to stay. She said the closest place was Gy. There was no way I could drag my head a further 20 kilometres today so I asked her for a taxi number. She said she would give me a lift in ten minutes. An hour later I got into her spaceship of a car and we drove to the outskirts of Gy.

It was a cold wet day and I arrived at the only hotel to find that it opened at 6pm. Everything else in the town was asleep as seems to be the case in France during August, so with three hours to fill I thought it was worth struggling up endless steps to an impressive château I could see at the top of the town. I entered the grand gates to a cobbled courtyard. The set-up was open to the public and I headed through every unlocked door on a self-guided tour. There was no one around although the last door I opened seemed to be someone's private house. I quickly tiptoed backwards before the man in the pantry turned around. By the time I was on the bottom step he was calling 'Mademoiselle'. He asked if I wanted to go round the château and I said yes. I paid him 4 euros, left my bag in his hall and went round the building again. I came back out into the pouring rain and went to shelter under the loggia of the town hall, looking blankly out between two Doric columns at a kebab van in the central square. As I focused I realised the owner was sitting in the front seat just staring back at me. I can't really be that interesting I thought as I shivered, longing for six o'clock. Tomorrow, whatever it took, I was going to make it to Besançon.

Gy - Besançon. August

I left Gy in pouring rain on a road through the dense forest, Grands Bois de Gy. It was early in the morning and I was full of excitement to reach Besançon. Well into the wood I saw a car coming towards me. As it got closer it slowed to a stop. The side window was wound down just as I passed and the overexcited driver stretched across his bewildered friend and shook my hand. I then shook the friend's hand and said 'Aujourd'hui Besançon'. They said 'Bon Voyage' and we both kept going. It was only afterwards that I realised the driver was the man who had charged me 4 euros for a second look at Gy Château.

Today was the furthest that I have walked in one day so far. I was too eager to reach Besançon to try to split the distance but 38 kilometres (plus getting rather lost in the outskirts) gave me soles sorer than I would have believed possible through just walking. The pain is really tender. Sitting down there is none but as soon as you put the slightest bit of weight on either foot it stretches across the entire sole and does not go away. It makes me walk incredibly slowly, furiously concentrating on ignoring it, but instead being totally preoccupied by it, and therefore getting very lost. I did not want to get my directions out to find my way to the centre of Besançon, as I could not cope with seeing the distance I was from it. So instead I somehow believed I could direct myself to the centre of somewhere I had never been having entered the outskirts from a field rather than the main road. Unsurprisingly I walked in a huge semi-circle through the northern council estates in the hot sunshine. Desperately needing the loo and sticking with sweat to the inside of my coat I stopped to take it off and look at my map. I then headed straight towards the biggest road on the map and found a café where I sat spaced out, for ages.

Feeling much better and armed with directions to the tourist office I headed off towards the centre. This is where I met the nicest of all tourist office women. I asked if there was any religious accommodation and she rushed back and forth from her computer and the telephone trying to find somewhere. Eventually, while I talked to a mother and her daughter (dressed totally in pink) about their holiday in Besançon, the helpful woman behind the desk said there was a room for me next door to the Cathedral as long as I was aged between 18 and 30. She told me it was over the river and right in the centre of the old town. Handing me an address and a telephone number she said she really hoped I could find it, as she had never heard of it before. I replied that I had found my way to her from Canterbury so wasn't worried. She smiled a little unsure if it really was a joke or not.

When I know I have a bed waiting for me I thoroughly enjoy the surprise of not knowing what it will be like or whom I will meet. I am so excited to get there and relieved to have a place to sleep that I give no thought to the superficial concerns such as if it is clean or dirty, frightening or homely. Instead I arrive with a broad smile and enthusiastic eyes no matter how sore my feet or tired my head. I thank those who give me a floor as much as those who give me a room in their house for free and in return I almost always receive a great big smile of warmth that I have no other way of getting unless I look in the mirror.

I easily found my way under the weathered 2nd century Porte Noire to the green door in an ivy-covered wall adjacent to la Cathédrale Saint-Jean. I buzzed the intercom and back came a French voice 'Oui'. I said 'Je suis un pèlerin' because I was incapable of saying 'the tourist office have recently rung you to ask if I could stay and, you having said yes, I am now here looking for a room.' Back came an indecipable gabble of French. Intercoms make understanding French even more difficult and, not being face to face, my pleading expression is no help and unintentionally I irritate the person on the other end. 'Je m'appelle Alice,' I said in the friendliest voice I could muster. Back came a furious rant from which I made out that it is holidays and no I can't stay. Unwilling to give up but not really sure what to do, I stood looking at the cobbled street. As if by chance the green door creaked on its hinges and a preoccupied nun barged past. Behind her was a woman of about my age smiling. She welcomed me in under an arch and pointed to her house above. In the door way we waved to her husband holding a grinning baby. I followed her across the courtyard and into a municipal-looking building where we wound up a huge concrete staircase past several gloomy landings to room No.17 on the top floor. There were five uncovered beds and a large rectangular window at the far end filled with the bell tower of the looming cathedral. I marched after her to be shown two showers and a loo at either end of the long dark corridor. We then rushed down a floor, along a corridor, round a corner, down some back stairs and into a large musty kitchen and telly room. Here she left me saying it must be kept locked. On my way back to the bedroom I passed a door with the sign *Accès Interdit*. Behind it was a room full of bed sheets, and a washing machine. Taking a pillowcase and bottom sheet for my bed I returned to room No.17, dug all my clothes out of my rucksack and raced back to put on a wash. The best part of a washing machine is the fresh smell of clean clothes which hand washing never seems to achieve.

After a long sleep I went to have a look around this seemingly uninhabited building I was in. I did not find much although a pin board in the hall suggests it is a place for young people with a residential community of two priests, two nuns, a few professionals and the young couple I had met who oversee everything. In the basement there was a modern chapel and on the door there was a note saying *Vespers 19h*. Sitting reading a pop-up version of the bible, I waited the ten minutes to seven o'clock. I then met the few other residents; two nuns both seemingly short of time and a goofy silent student, David, who was almost too shy even to shake my hand. Once the young couple and their baby Marc had arrived we all sat in a row singing to no music. It is my third sitting of Vespers in French but still I find it hard to follow the words. I now know that at a particular point we all sing a sentence one after the other. I am far too shy to join in and remaining silent when it is my turn results in the person next to me taking on the responsibility.

With a day off tomorrow I could finally risk the fatigue and take myself out to dinner. I found my way to a tiny street full of restaurants and people drinking rosé at tables on the pavement. I went inside what seemed the busiest of them all and ate an average salad and a caramel waffle and didn't really enjoy any of it. People like to stare when you are alone which I would not mind if they smiled as well but they give off a sense that they are wary of you and this makes me feel pretty isolated. Little did I know that this was nothing compared to being alone in Italy.

After a sound night's sleep, a late rise and delicious breakfast in a small side street I went to get my pilgrim passport stamped at the Cathedral. The two women behind the desk were thrilled to meet someone doing such a large pilgrimage and they could not have been sweeter. They wanted to touch me and of course I let them hold an arm each for a bit. It was so funny.

In Besançon Cathedral is a room with the most phenomenal clock. Six times a day, a professorial-looking man, dressed in a suit black enough for a funeral, gives a presentation in French. Holding a yardstick in the manner of a magic wand he goes into a hugely elaborate description of many different aspects of the clock, getting so engrossed in the act of his presentation that it would be no surprise if he performed every hour regardless of whether he had an audience or not.

The clock, which is 5.80 metres high and 2.5 metres wide, is housed in a room of the Cathedral spire. It is wonderful with 70 dials showing 122 indications which include the local time of 17 places around the world, times and heights of the tides in 8 different French ports, the seasons, leap year cycles, motions and orbits of the planets, the days of the week, the months of the year and times of sunset and sunrise. On the hour, every hour, the ropes ring the bells, and during various times statues of apostles come and go and angels turn around. I had timed my visit perfectly as when the clock struck noon Mary, standing on the crest of the clock, lowered her sceptre, a coffin opened and Christ rose from it. His resurrection is short-lived because he is apparently buried again at 3 pm. The whole construction, built by Auguste-Lucien in the nineteenth century, consists of more than 30,000 pieces. Today it remains worth every second of going to look at it.

After an afternoon of sleep in bed or sitting topless in the spot of sunshine on the wooden floor, at six o'clock I went to Mass in the church of Sainte Madeleine. Having realised during Mass in Laon that I was in fact walking to Rome for God helped me so much when I was finding it particularly difficult. When in despair I questioned what on earth I was doing, I would look up at the space between the ground and the sky and remind myself I was doing it for God. This responsibility gave me no option but to carry on and by doing so I knew in return I was living a wonderful journey. However, as the days of thought accumulated, I was upsetting myself by struggling to identify the path I was going to follow for the rest of my life. With a day off in Besançon I had to go to Mass. It is not that I expected to get an answer but by being in church where no one judges one, one can let everything go and give in to the depth of one's feelings. I found that by the time Mass was over I felt a lot better than when it had started. For me this process only happened during the service – sitting in a church when nothing is going on did not have the same intensity about it.

During Mass in Besançon I cried a lot and felt so woozy that I could not stand up for most of it, but I knew from the moment I walked out that I would write a book about this walk and then I would pursue life as an artist. I had no idea about the story of the book but, by being disciplined and writing every day, I hoped that when the journey ended I would see it all clearly.

On my final night in Besançon the resident young couple, Amélie and Jerome, invited me to dinner. We sat outside on plastic chairs round a table-clothed table with olives, crisps, bread, wine and martini. It was great to be a part of this, mainly because only chance could have brought me here. Amélie and Jerome were easygoing, such good people and their baby Marc was the cheeriest child I had ever seen. He was always beaming, never whining or craving attention, just content to be amongst others. Jerome was lanky, unshaven and had the aura of an architect; Amélie dark, tall, very thin but with wide hips, almost gypsy-like though with pale skin. They were unobviously religious and had met through their church group.

Slowly some of their friends arrived. Initially, a couple in their first month of marriage, a young girl with a strong character but putty in the hands of an apparently older husband. He was so thin I thought he was gay but as the evening progressed he undoubtedly had an eye for women. His English was by far the best and despite his wife's attentions—endlessly getting up to kiss him and ending up on his knee with a blanket over them both—he had an enticingly flirtatious manner.

Not long after the couple arrived, a large self-absorbed character with a beard turned up. He sat muttering and chuckling to himself rather than interact with the rest of us. He had brought with him a half-eaten polenta and spinach tart as well as his salad spinner full of lettuce and clover. We all tucked in under the stars and eventually in candlelight, chatting about themes for their future parties. When I got up to go to bed they could not have been nicer about what I was up to. We all kissed and said goodbye with them telling me I must write a book and if I needed somewhere to do it I could come back and live there.

Besançon - Étalans. August

The next day I left early along the River Doubs, an oxbow of which encloses the old town and centre of Besançon. The humidity caused a mist to rise off it. Leaving the banks of the river I climbed up a steep hill and over into countryside that whispered that the border of Switzerland is near. The air was cool, the sky blue, the sun bright, the fields and woods lush and green which, without permanent rain, surprised me. I mostly walked along rocky tracks past lazy cows with huge bells round their necks. I did not see a single other person until I reached Étalans, where I spent a nervous night.

I made my way down the cul-de-sac with a scruffy building at the end, outside which sat four pot-bellied men chewing on rolled-up cigarettes and looking into lip-stained wine glasses. They said something to me but I just smiled as I bent under the doorway and entered the bar. Off to my right was a room full of similar types sitting at long tables. The place went quiet and everyone's eyes were on me. From behind the bar Madame stuck out her hand to shake mine. I asked if there was a room and saying something she pointed at the ceiling. Showing her my watch I asked what time lunch was finishing. 'Maintenant,' she replied. I then asked about dinner to which she replied 'Pas de dîner.' So, in a corner of a room full of drunks, sombre on large bottles of unlabeled wine, I sat flicking away the flies and feeling as hungry as I was thirsty. I ate whatever came, resisting the half eaten bits of bread that were on the table before I arrived. The whole room was watching me but no one was sober enough to return my smile.

I reached Madame to pay for the room and lunch by squeezing past three dirty large men at the bar who were drinking whisky out of coffee cups. Up a wooden staircase on the outside of the building and on to a landing with tubs of paint and rollers obstructing the corridor I made my way to the only door with a key in it. If I knew where I was spending the night I would not have come, but as it was, with no dinner served in the bar, I felt happier here in an empty building than I did on the night when I was barred into a cell in Brienne-le-Château. I washed in a dirty shower down one end of the corridor and got into bed already looking forward to leaving the next day.

It took me a long time to get to sleep. I attempted to read but my head wasn't up for it, so instead I tried our childhood method of lying incredibly still. Just as I was drifting off there was an almighty clatter followed by voices of gruff men fumbling keys in doors and then someone falling over with such a thud it made my shutters quiver. I finally slept mulling over the thought that if I was going to be raped then this was surely the place.

Étalans - Ouhans. August

The worst part of my night was the unbelievably runny tummy I had the next day. I was heading to Ouhans and thankfully I followed a road by the side of a wood most of the way. Almost every other step until my loo paper ran out, I had to dart into the woods and squat rather too close to the road behind a tree. It happened so many times I took my photograph to see how pale I had gone. It crossed my mind it might be the tap water in my pack so I rationed myself to sips only taken when feeling faint. Nevertheless I made the 29 kilometres to Ouhans, finding strength glancing back at the unending view of the kilometres that I have now covered.

Having checked in to the only hotel in the town and been asleep for a good hour, I went downstairs to get a packet of crisps from the bar. Going back to my room I followed a hot, slow-moving woman carrying a rucksack and two walking poles. 'Do you speak English?' I asked. 'Yeah, I sure do,' replied a West Coast American accent. 'I'm Pam, we've' — pointing to three other ladies on the landing we had now reached — 'walked from Canterbury and we're going all the way to Rome.' 'That is fantastic,' I said. 'I'm Alice and I've also come from Canterbury.' 'Gee Alice, that's just great. Let's have dinner together. 8 o'clock suit you?' 'I'd love to have dinner but can we make it 7:30?' 'Sure, sweetie, we can do that, can't we, girls?' 'Sure, Alice,' they all replied, 'see you then.'

Ouhans - Pontarlier. August

By the time I left the next day I felt the Americans and I had known each other for days. Aged between 66 and 73, they were all very different characters. One so chatty no one else got to finish what they were saying, one looked slightly African and kept herself happy referencing everything to her ipad, one was sensitive but never got the opportunity to say what she was thinking so winked instead, and another, Wanda, every so often made a point rather suddenly and loudly.

They all dress as though for skiing, and their large silhouettes are quite a sight, shuffling along and capped with drawstring hats. Laden with bags, poles, GPS, iphone, ipad, taking it slowly but getting there. They were inclusive and had a casual air about them, which was easy to slot into. I enjoyed their company but soon I left them behind. The enthusiasm to reach Pontarlier, where I would spend my final night in France, quickened my pace.

I was excited by the prospect of Switzerland that I had read was the most beautiful part of the Via Francigena. This southern part of France was much prettier than the vast cereal fields of the north but the rolling valleys, full forests, fecund gardens, verges blooming with wild flowers, pale blue sky and dream-like wisps of white clouds did nothing to fill the gap left from the warmth and kindness of the humble people I stumbled across in Northern France.

Pontarlier – Vuiteboeuf. August

Having walked for thirty-three days I crossed the silent border into Switzerland. I had got up very early and was on top of the mountain as the mist was still rising from the valley and it felt as if the rest of the world was asleep. There were no animals, people, or cars, just a derelict border control building which looked a bit like an old-fashioned petrol station. On one gable there was a French flag, on another a Swiss. I sat on a bench on a mound of very green Swiss grass and ate a pain au chocolat.

I rang Muma who is amazingly good at living other people's excitement. At moments like this when I know I should be excited I get bogged down in listening to my feelings and thinking that perhaps I should be more excited than I am. I wanted to hear the joy in Muma's voice. It made my day and I felt I could walk forever.

On I went climbing high up to 1600 metres in the Jura Mountains before descending to Sainte-Croix where, longing for a strong drink, I stopped for a celebratory cup of coffee. On my way into the bar I tripped on the step and with my backpack still on went flying sideways into a table of two men. I got chatting to them and when I came to leave they paid my bill. Suddenly I felt welcomed into a country I didn't even know how to say hello in.

Switzerland made me feel uneasy. The mountains are tall and sharp and lined from head to toe with pointy fir trees. Every so often a gap in the trees reveals a nauseating drop and it is as if one is looking down from an airplane with the window open. It is pretty breathtaking but I prefer our far less daunting little green valley and rolling hills in South West Scotland. The skiing villages, whose signs, unlike Christmas decorations, remain up out of season, look bare without snow in the streets and the people kick about with little to do. Heading down from Sainte Croix I was on such a steep path on my right hand side that I felt too queasy to stop and eat the baguette in my bag. I could see way down to the Swiss Mittelland, which stretched east to Yverdon-les-Bains and Lac de Neuchâtel and south to Lac Léman and the Swiss Alps blocking the view in the distance. They are monstrous beings in their own right and the thought of going over them began to frighten me. As soon as I got to the bottom of the Jura Mountains and safely onto flat ground I stopped for the night in the first hotel I came to.

There was Internet in my room and I spent several hours searching for somewhere to stay between here, Vuiteboeuf, and Lausanne. I struggled to find anywhere and decided tomorrow I would walk east to Yverdon-les-Bains and get on a train to Lausanne. I slept lightly as the breeze carried the rattle of cows' bells into my room and woke to the heaviest rain I have ever seen.

Vuiteboeuf - Lausanne. August

It was too wet to get out my hopelessly large-scale map so instead, carrying my compass in front of me, I cut my own path to Yverdon-les-Bains. After stopping several bewildered people on the way I arrived absolutely drenched at the central station. It is not a nice feeling dipping into public transport. Suddenly one is no longer a pilgrim but just a pitiful dirty traveller. One feels self-conscious and there is no satisfaction in arriving at one's destination.

Lausanne stretches uphill from the shore of Lac Léman, the largest freshwater lake in central Europe. I struggled up the steep narrow streets towards the medieval city centre to go and have a look at the Cathédrale de Notre-Dame which sits at the highest point of the city. As a result of the Reformation's destruction of any symbolism or decoration that hinted at idolatry, the inside of this architecturally decorative cathedral is very plain. A few frescoes and sculptures survived but overall it remains an austere space. Unintentionally I found my way to a catholic church where Mass in Italian was about to begin. A little old woman who appeared to live in a room just off the entrance let me leave my bag resting against her desk as I entered the church. It was the first Italian I had heard, such a flamboyant language that you feel it should only really be spoken by grown-ups. As the Mass went on I felt as if I was watching an orchestra-less opera of a man confessing his unrequited love. There were not many people in the congregation but I hovered around in the hall afterwards hoping someone might offer me a bed. Unfortunately not, and the cross-eyed woman with whom I had left my bag could not suggest anywhere apart from the youth hostel which, when she rang it, was full. I left and went in search of a tourist office.

The middle-aged woman in the tourist office could hardly have been more unhelpful. Her suggestion for finding a bed in Lausanne was to look on the Internet. I said I was walking and she got out a large paper map and began circling Internet cafes. I was not up for squeezing into an Internet café so I asked if she had a list of accommodation to which she replied by handing me a booklet full of addresses in such a way that you would think her desperate to talk to the next person in the queue. I then asked about accommodation outside Lausanne for the next few days but it seems they have absolutely no information outside Lausanne.

I stood under the shelter of a bus stop going down the list of prices and circled the cheapest ones. After traipsing from one to another to another, all with big notices saying 'No Vacancies', I looked down the price of hotels. I went to the one closest to me and asked the receptionist what was her absolutely cheapest room. 67 euros which considering the average hostel was 50 euros I thought a bargain. Her English was good so we chatted for twenty minutes or so as I was in need of some company. She was intrigued by my walk and said I could sneak into breakfast tomorrow morning and that way I would have a good start to a new day. I got in the lift and went up to an amazingly comfy clean room with a bath and a shower.

Lausanne - Villeneuve. August

At 6.30 a.m. I filled up on the buffet breakfast and spent the day walking the whole of the way round one side of Lac Léman into the village of Villeneuve at the far point. Apart from a few steep climbs into the Larvaux terraces, which cut across the hills that roll up from the northern shore of Lac Léman, I mostly walked along paved paths on the lakeshore. I walked past joggers, glamorous dog walkers, short piers and white-washed holiday homes. The whole day had a Californian feel to it. As the hours passed the grey sky gave way to a huge expanse of pale blue and the sun shone glistening off the water. All day I looked forward to a swim.

By midday the only clouds left in the sky were the ones lingering like dog collars round the necks of the now visible high, high mountains of the Dents du Midi to the South and the Swiss Alps of the Rhone valley to the East. They are like a barrier in the distance, a daunting sight and certainly the highest peaks I have ever seen. I would say that the view was beautiful but for the dread that was building up inside me that I had to go over them. As I climbed through the terraced vines above Vervay and past the famous Château de Chillon on its rocky island something pulled in the back of my left knee and a shooting pain went down my shin and into my left foot. At the time it was almost unbearable to put any weight on but after walking it off slowly it seemed to get manageable enough to continue so I put on my headphones to drown out the pain and cruised through Montreux all the way to the end of the lake smiling with happiness in my bubble of pop music. Having reached Villeneuve, an old-fashioned town and the last on the northern banks of Lac Léman, I changed in a public loo into my floral swimming costume and, leaving my rucksack close to the water, I waded in and eased off my tired legs. Longing to lie in bed I got dressed over the wet costume and went to find a place to stay.

Having booked into a small hotel and struggled to sleep, hunger sent me in search of somewhere to eat. I entered a restaurant by the lake, which had a sign on the door saying *FOOD SERVED ALL DAY.* I ate on a jetty into the lake sitting at a table with a blue cover under a blue and white awning. The sun was still hot, I could hear the water lapping over the top of burbling conversations. One after another small birds were enjoying flying beneath the awning and the Germans amongst us would squawk and thrash out an arm to get rid of them. I have never eaten horse before and because I doubted I would ever be on a jetty into Lac Léman again I thought I would eat something I never normally would. It was very chewy and the more you chew it the more of a tight woollen ball it becomes. Swallowing feels like you are not meant to be doing it and the lump slugs down your oesophagus like a dense tasteless mass.

Looking west down the glistening lake I wished I could stay up for the sunset, which looked so good there might not be another day to come.

Villeneuve - Saint-Maurice. August

When something is very sore it is almost impossible to think or concentrate on anything else. The only exception is when you are frightened to death by what you are doing and then, despite pain, all you can feel is an isolated heart beat. But today I felt pain the whole way to Saint-Maurice. On my way to dinner on the jetty last night my left big toe was too sore to stand on and I had to hobble with the weight on the side of my foot. This morning the whole of my left foot from the bone in the big toe right over the arch was incredibly sore. As the day went on the pain spread up my ankle and into my shin. I stopped a lot to massage it and eventually ended up walking with a tubi-grip stretched from my knee to my toes. The only time I got any relief from the pain was sitting on a rock dangling my legs into the fast flowing glacial river Rhone.

As I ambled out of Villeneuve I said bonjour to a man walking past me. He turned around and gave me a grin as if to say I'm keen if you are. As I reached the other end of the street about to exit the town a car pulled up by my side. The window went down and from across the passenger seat the man I had said hello to asked me where I was going. 'Saint-Maurice' I replied. Patting the passenger seat he said 'I take you, get in, très jolie, très jolie, très jolie.' Smiling I said 'Je marche'. He then began kissing the air several times in a row before saying 'bises, bises, bises'. Feeling the heat in my cheeks I said 'non merci' and walked on with my head down.

Sauntering along the flat river path I passed many unfriendly bicyclists, however the strong smell of aftershave that wafted after them was intoxicatingly delicious. They were dressed as if taking part in a race and going so fast they might as well have been on a machine in the gym. Walking alone and slower than those who use hiking poles, I feel that I live every step, noticing all that is going on around me. Today the sky was full of helicopters, looping-the-loop little planes, aeroplanes, gliders and huge white clouds puffing out from a big chimney. There is a lot of industry stuffed up this valley; trucks, warehouses, cranes, chimneys, electricity grids, pylons, all dwarfed by the huge, steep mountains but hideous all the same.

Goodness knows how but I managed to get lost following the river. Unlike yesterday when I ended up jumping from one boulder island to another around the edge of Lac Léman, having read 'hug the shore of the lake' too literally, today, preoccupied with pain, I had veered away from the river and arrived at the barriers of a motorway. When you are walking and find you are lost, the one thing you have no desire to do is retrace your steps. So, knowing the river was somewhere to my right I decided to cut across a field of giant maize. I picked an alley through the middle and made my way up it feeling as if I had shrunk. At the far end there was no space between the maize and an unruly wood. Even more determined not to have to retrace my steps I thrashed through the thick spikey mass. I did think to myself it was a bit crazy, however it felt intrepid and my stick was a great help in pushing down a path through the brambles. Just as I was getting concerned that I could not hear the river I came across a wet clay path. Slipping my way along it, adding to the weight of my sore leg, I came out on a much bigger track. I chose to turn left and reappeared next to the motorway. Giving in, I retraced my steps to where I had joined the track and this time turned right. Thankfully it led me back to the river. Carrying no food, I did not dare take any pain-killers on an empty tummy and instead went all the way to the Abbey at Saint-Maurice with my mouth tight shut with pain and all my thoughts on my foot. The sky was completely blue and with the sun shining bright I hoped so much that it would be like this when I have to climb to the

Col du Grand St-Bernard[3]. I crossed the Rhone by an ancient bridge built in the 12th century into the medieval town of Saint-Maurice, nestled into the side of a cliff.

The secretary, smelling of stale cigarettes, told me there would be a Canon arriving at four-thirty to show me to my room. I noticed two other rucksacks in the hall and asked the woman if they were pilgrims. 'Oui,' she replied, two Belgians. I asked if they were men. They were. I asked if they were young and the telephone rang. I thought perhaps whilst waiting for a room in an Abbey it wasn't the right time to show excitement at the possibility that they might be young, so leaving my bag with theirs I went in search of a chemist. I did my usual non-drowsy act to the pharmacist and she gave me the strongest ibuprophen as well as a packet of 1000g paracetamol.

When four-thirty came a beguiling little man with a cross round his neck led me and the Belgian couple into our rooms within this ancient Abbey, founded in 515. Lacking energy to wash my clothes I decided to shower in them instead. I was eager to go to Mass at six and when the time came I could not open the heavy vaulted door outside my room. There was a knob to unlock but it simply would not budge. I got so hot trying, my fingers began to slip rather than turn. I returned to my room and telephoned the Abbey. Of course everyone was at Mass except the secretary who could not understand me but thankfully came outside. I hung out of the window shouting 'bonjour madame' down the street. She came to me and I pointed down at the door, which she made her way through.

At times, it really surprises me how, since hitting my head, I have lost the ability to think round a problem. I just simply don't think or even think about thinking. I closed the door behind the secretary and asked her to open it. Rather bemused by my request, I watched as she pushed it in on itself and then turned the knob. I rushed to Mass feeling very stupid.

---

[3] At 8000 ft above sea level, the Great St Bernard Pass is Switzerland's highest pass, lying on the ridge between the two highest summits of the Alps, Mont Blanc and Monte Rosa.

Bizarrely I wasn't very hungry as I sat down to dinner with the Belgian couple but I actually think it was because for only the third time in 37 days I had people to talk to. We were in what seemed more like a sitting room than a dining room, at the end of a long dark stone corridor. The woman spoke good English and despite not talking I am sure her husband understood it. He was a frail old man with big features and a particularly intriguing mouth. He had a very thin arch to the top of it causing his teeth to stick out like a jumble of tombstones which, with his lips pulled over them, gave him a permanent smile. There was something so endearing about it that I would speak at him in English so as to make him smile even more.

Halfway through dinner the little man who had shown us to our rooms came in and sat down while we ate. He had a strange manner, as if preoccupied by his own thoughts; however, I enjoyed the challenge of trying to make friends. He has been a Canon in the Abbey since he was 22 and he was now 72. The Belgians were nice but totally impersonal. Even at three o'clock in the morning when the wind was howling and something was banging and we all ended up—me in my nighty and them in t-shirts with knickers and droopy thin brown old legs below—fumbling around the dark corridor trying to find out the cause of the noise, they barely said a thing. When I brought it up at breakfast they brushed it off when in fact it was very funny, both the scene and the coincidence, that we all got up at the same time.

I have recently passed half-way but failed to remember to take in when it was or take a photograph. Knowing now that I have passed half-way is not as good as you might think. Before starting I knew the distance to Rome was 2083 kilometres but, having never worked in kilometres before, that figure was rather abstract. It is only when you reach half-way that the magnitude of the journey hits you. This is not a happy thought and I now wished I did not know. Unlike the weight in my rucksack there was no way of getting rid of any kilometres. What's more I was pretty sure I would get lost again and therefore the distance was even greater. What I was yet to discover is how much harder the distance becomes the less it gets.

Saint-Maurice - Orsières. August

As I got further into the mountains I became more and more nervous of them and just longed to be up, over and out of the Alps forever. I really did not like being alone amongst such frightening giants whose fallen rocks in the valley were bigger than apple trees. I left Saint-Maurice early and went on a route via the famous Pissevache waterfall whose former beauty artists have been inspired to record in words or paintings. Today its great force powers a hydroelectric power plant at the base but for me there was still something special to see. Through the trees and up the wooden walk-way, there was the waterfall, with a rainbow arching across the base of it. No one else was around, I took off my rucksack, climbed over the wooden gallery up on to a big rock directly beneath the dropping silver gush and standing in the spray I grasped at the weightless spectrum.

As I passed through Martigny, the last big town this side of the Alps, on my way to Sembrancher where I planned to spend the night, I decided to go to the tourist office and ask if they had any useful maps or booklets on walking in the mountains. Although they did not have anything to give me, the sympathetic woman told me that the path between Martigny and Sembrancher was very dangerous due to erosion and not safe to go on alone particularly with a large rucksack. With even more fear inside me I headed to the train station.

I did not once look out of the window. I took the train for ten kilometres and sat in a seat with my boots off massaging my foot which having been bound up this morning was much less sore than yesterday. When I arrived in Sembrancher I decided that despite having walked 16 kilometres this morning I easily had the determination to walk the 8.4 kilometres to Orsières. Although it meant an ascent of 183 metres it would thankfully get me a day closer to the Col du Grand St-Bernard.

It was such a hot day that the first time on this journey I felt my skin burning. Somehow on my way to Orsières I managed once again to lose track of the directions and ended up climbing much higher than I needed to. Baking hot and running low on water I saw the town far below me in the valley. I found a steep track through trees and coming across a stream I stopped to bathe my extremely sore soles. The water was ice cold, which helps so much with the pain and keeps the swelling of my left foot down. Concern for my left foot made me determined to reach the Col du Grand St-Bernard tomorrow for fear of the pain getting worse with time. I knew this was the most physically challenging part of the route and I wanted to give myself the best chance before my foot gave in.

I arrived in the main square of Orsières opposite a smart hotel. It was after two o'clock but outside sat a few people still having lunch. Knowing it would cost a fortune I sat down and thought of it like my last supper. I ordered plates of the most delicious sophisticated food and decided if tomorrow was as dangerous as I imagined then I was going to eat in celebration of my life. The table became covered in food and I smiled with glee as the people around me turned to look, not one of them even nodding hello. The slim French fries were perfectly crunchy, the toasted granary baguette kept warm in a wicker basket, the butter as pale and milky as the cows, a salad with the freshest array of leaves sprinkled with pine nuts and shavings of sweet crunchy radishes. Best of all was the steak tartare topped with strong parmesan and flat leaf parsley on a plate decorated with spots of balsamic syrup and a pureed avocado squiggle. It was absolutely delicious. I tasted each mouthful and filled my senses with delight rather than apprehension.

After lunch I went in search of a place to stay. I knocked on a door opposite the church and a priest with a huge smile opened it. He came out and led me into a building nearby. It had two floors each with a long table and benches. The walls were decorated with scraps of Sunday school drawings. There was a mattress on the floor upstairs and two downstairs. In broken English he told me that there was no loo but there are some public ones in the car park on the other side of the church. I asked about a shower and he said if I didn't tell anyone I could use his seeing as I was alone. Back we went to the house he had come out of and he showed me the way to his bathroom.

I made as cosy a bed as I could on the mattress upstairs and having showered I went to look for the tourist office in hopes of finding out some more information on walking in the Alps. It was shut, there was no sign on the door, and it looked as if it had not been open for some time. Having seen me trying to go in, the man in the shop next door came out. In my best French I tried to explain to him that tomorrow I was walking to the Col du Grand St-Bernard and I was looking for a map. He walked me down the road to a wooden sign post which said *Gt St Bernard Summit 7h 15m*. Pointing at the sign he said 'C'est facile, c'est facile. Non mappa.' I thanked him and was slightly relieved by what I understood to be his insistence that it was easy following the signs. Off I went to buy food and extra water for the big day tomorrow.

When I came back to my bed for the night two other pilgrims had turned up. They were both old men, one French and one Dutch, also walking to Rome having started in Reims. The Dutchman, Jan, spoke good English but neither of them were particularly friendly and both lacked energy in their demeanour. As Claude, the Frenchman, unpacked his things, Jan and I discussed tomorrow. He was unsure whether they would make it all the way to the Hospice du Grand-Saint-Bernard or whether they would follow the road and spend the night half way in Bourg-Saint-Pierre. I said I was so nervous I wanted to get it all over and done with in one day and was going to leave at six-thirty in the morning. He made a careless face and said they would be leaving after me. I went to bed more frightened by the prospect of tomorrow than anything else about the whole journey.

Orsières - Col du Grand St-Bernard. August

I had recurring nightmares of falling down scree off the alpine paths. Waking three times desperate for the loo, I had to drag myself out past the church under the bright stars of the clear night sky to the dirty public loos. At 5:30am my heart was pounding and I could sleep no more and by 6:30 I was on my way, following the signs the man had pointed out. To begin with I was consoled by the fact they led me up the same path as my guidebook. I had a bag full of food and water, the sun was out and there were enough clouds in the sky to shade the heat.

Within an hour my book diverted off the track; however, the marker post of the signs I have been following now said 7h to the summit. Knowing I walk quicker than average I decided this would be a shorter route and continued on up the track. At a fork with a tarmac road two hours further on the sign no longer said *Gt. St. Bernard Summit* so I took a guess and turned to the right. Twenty minutes later a car came towards me and I flagged it down. I asked the woman driving if this was the way to the 'Col du Grand St-Bernard'. She told me I needed to go back down the road and take the fork to the left. Much to my relief the next sign I came to read *Gt. St. Bernard Summit*. I was so nervous that day that at times when I would have usually stopped to eat I had no urge to and just continued walking as the hours passed, longing to have arrived safely. I went up and up and up the side of a steep empty valley. I was exhausted but kept reminding myself that only in February I could not stand alone and had to be pushed to the loo in a chair with a hole in the seat and now I could walk further than I had ever dreamed of being capable of doing. I was way above the tree line, following the direction of the sparsely spaced wooden signs. There was no obvious path, no people, no animals and no houses. It was completely silent and I could see nothing other than a dropping valley behind me and a barrier of huge sharp peaks in front. Each time I passed a sign it settled my heartbeat and then as the distance from one sign to another grew larger so the beat of my heart gained in weight against my chest. Although I was on the shady side of the valley I dripped with sweat and despite several streams I was reluctant to lighten my load and get rid of the excess water I was carrying. Eventually, having walked uphill non-stop for three and a half hours, still with high peaks in front of me, I came to a marker post which read *Gt. St. Bernard Summit 3h 40m*. Reassured that I had passed half way, I collapsed on the ground. Lying against the steepness of the slope I ate half the contents of my food stores. I had not realised until I began eating how much I was craving sugar. The food went down with pure purpose rather than pleasure and I lay restless waiting for the glucose to kick in. Full of apprehension I headed on up towards one of many sharp peaks. Although there was no path it seemed obvious that I had to traverse one side of the steep valley at a gradual ascent. Longing for another sign it was half an hour before I came to two forking marker posts and neither of them said *Gt. St. Bernard Summit.* One pointed on up the valley, which was now becoming more of a vertical climb and the other pointed left across a rocky plain towards an even higher peak. I got out my hopelessly large-scale road map and tried to work out where on earth I was. I could see absolutely nothing to give me any orientation other than a tiny stream that had been parallel to me in the lower parts of the valley. Taking this as my bearing meant that the Col du Grand St-Bernard was surprisingly far to my left. Even if I was slightly out, heading left seemed to be more in the correct direction. I crossed the plain and with no more markers I aimed for the summit knowing that at least on top I would have a better view. From here on in I prayed and I prayed. I must have said more Hail Marys today than most people would have time to say during the whole of their life. I felt hollow with fear. As I climbed past lonely patches of snow the face became even more vertical than it looked from afar. The ground was loose under my feet and I knew what I was going up was too steep to come down, but I just had to get to the peak in the hope their would be a sign on the top. I pulled myself up with my hands onto the very narrow bridge between two dangerously steep drops. There was no sign and the view in front of me was one of such terror I could not bring myself to look up again. I got out my camera and without looking at the screen I photographed where I had come from and what I was facing. I then took a picture of myself, which I had absolutely no desire to look at. I was standing on a stone plaque that read *2978m La Tsavre Mt. Ferret.* A raindrop fell and I knew that whatever it took I had to find a valley with civilisation. I put on my waterproof and, bracing myself, looked again at the view that had winded me with terror. There, far below, I could see the lush green tone of the bottom of the valley. I sat down and in my shorts I slid over the top and down the scree slowing the speed with my less sore right foot until I reached firmer ground. I stood up, ignoring the blood weeping out of my grazed legs. I was now near enough to see the pin-prick of what looked like a farmhouse. I did not care where the Col du Grand St-Bernard was; I just knew I had to get to that farmhouse. I went down the mountain face which was so steep you would not believe me if I pointed it out. I was incredibly frightened knowing that one slip of either foot would send me tumbling down, down, down a lethal slope. Carefully, getting as much grip as possible on the side of the mountain with my hands, I slowly, slowly descended. Every so often I would dare to glance down at the lush green patch my mind was focused on. As it came nearer I saw a group of people walking up along the bottom of the valley. I was desperate to get to them and tried as hard as I could to move at a safe enough but fast enough speed to intercept them. Constantly glancing down to clock their progress I saw they had stopped to take each other's photograph. I now prayed they would stop long enough for me to reach them. As I hit the dirt track in the valley bottom the group were resting on a rock by my side.

Rushing my words I asked 'Do you speak English?' When I heard the word 'Yes' it was such an enormous relief I had to stop myself from bursting into uncontrollable tears. I dumped my rucksack, stripped my sticky waterproof off my baking body and pointing behind me I said, 'I've just come over that'. They looked up with utter amazement and then one man pointed to tell me I had cut my legs. Big deal, I thought as I bent down trying to wipe off the now crusty blood. I told them I had not meant to come over it but that I was lost and was in fact trying to get to the Hospice at the Col du Grand St-Bernard. They unfolded their map and said it would take me five hours from here and that I had to go up over a ridge and into an adjacent valley. One man pointed up the valley we were in to a ridiculously high peak saying 'it's somewhere over the top of there'. At that moment I gave in and thought stuff the Col du Grand St-Bernard. I told them I was too exhausted and they said if I walked down the track for half an hour I would get to Ferret where I could catch a bus. I thanked God over and over again as I walked down the track, disappointed with my naïve irresponsibility but greatly relieved I was safe.

Ferret was a village with very few houses, one bar and a bus stop. I went to the bar and chatted to the man behind it who spoke good

English. He told me the next bus was in two hours so instead I asked if he knew anyone I could pay to take me to the Hospice du Grand St Bernard. He said no but that a lot of people hitch-hike and I could try that. Heading outside I met an Italian family who were just arriving. Their son spoke English and I asked if after lunch they would give me a lift. He pointed at their small car and said 'no space'. I tried to explain I would squeeze in the boot but they found me more of a nuisance than an amusement so I headed back up the road to the bus stop. I sat on a bench eating fizzy peach rings and every time a car came past, which was not often, I would leap up and stick my thumb out. Not one of them stopped. I even asked a man delivering a parcel to one of the few houses if he would give me a lift but he pretended not to understand me.

The truth is, had I got out my road map, despite its large scale, I would have realised it was a very long way in a car from where I was to the Hospice du Grand St-Bernard. I was still in shock from what I had just done and blocking it out of my mind, even to the point of not looking at a map to see where I was. Actually, it didn't even cross my mind to look at a map and see where I was. For some reason I thought the Summit was close by and if I could not get a lift there I would just get on the bus when it eventually came. If I thought about it I would have realised that the track I had walked down to the village and the one I would have taken if I had wanted to cross over to the adjacent valley was not fit for cars let alone a bus. It was obvious if you thought about it but I didn't think. I sat happy with the thought that I was safe and, though not on foot, I was still going to get to the Hospice at the Col Grand St-Bernard today.

Much to my surprise the bus arrived at two o'clock, half an hour early. I was very excited and rushed, even though there was no one else around, to get on it. As I was climbing the steps the fat driver stood up as if to get out so I stepped backwards. Out he wobbled and stood rather too close to me. 'Bonjour' I grinned. 'Bonjour' he said in a gruff voice. We had as much of a conversation as we could with a struggle to understand each other's accents. He was not going anywhere for half an hour and when I said I wanted to go to the

Col du Grand St-Bernard he looked at me with a heavy brow and said 'Non?' I eventually understood with the help of his bus timetable that this valley did not connect to the valley with the Col du Grand St-Bernard and that to get a bus I was going to have to go all the way back to Orsières and then go up the right valley. The problem was this man's bus did not go to Orsières and it was too late in the day to catch the connecting bus at the next stop. As tomorrow is Saturday and buses do not run this high up in the mountains at the weekend I would have to wait until Monday to begin trying to get three connecting buses to the Summit. I stood looking at him with an exaggerated helpless face hoping he would solve my problem. He did not seem at all bothered so when he turned to me as if he had a brain-wave of a solution, my ears pricked up, and he told me I should walk there. I did my best to tell him about my day but totally understandably he did not believe a word and just kept pointing up the track saying 'Quatre heures, quatre heures, c'est facile, c'est facile'. I told him I was all alone and asked if it was dangerous. He stuck out his hand horizontally, fingers together and made a steep slope and then said 'un peu', before flattening his hand to a gradual ascent saying 'C'est facile.' I looked at him as if questioning what he was saying. Time was running out and I needed to make a decision.

I walked up the track at great speed knowing I had to give myself as many daylight hours as possible to get there. I was now on the sunny side of the valley on a wide track that went up at a gradual ascent. I continued to pray but I was now confident that this route would take me all the way to the Summit. After an hour the track just stopped. It was as if it had gone up the valley as far as it could bear and then run out of steam for the steepness of the slope it suddenly faced. There was a marker post, similar to the ones I had followed this morning and to my relief, although I was also sceptical, it said *Gt. St. Bernard Summit 3h 45m* and pointed to the left up the steepest slope in sight. Knowing I had now missed the bus I continued with rapid Hail Mary's one after the other as I climbed and climbed the steepest path fit for walkers. The rocks were huge and the narrow path zigzagged its way between them up the face of a mountain. I do not know how

I did it. I was so utterly exhausted I had to link my hands under each knee alternately and lift my legs one at a time in front of each other. Without doing this I was incapable of lifting my foot high enough to keep climbing at such a steep angle. I drew in breaths so deep my throat hurt and my skin stung with sweat. I stopped, my chest welled up with fear and I just did not know if I could go on any more. Looking up I saw the brow of a peak and, telling myself this was the last climbing I had to do, I mustered the energy to get to the top. In front of me I could see a huge lake with the group who had helped me sitting by the side. I went to raise my arms in the air but could not lift them above my shoulders. I called out and they all turned around and stood up with surprise throwing their arms in the air. I walked towards them and without stopping I dumped my rucksack, took off my boots and waded straight into the lake cupping the water in my hands and throwing it over my head. This was the maddest day of my life. I felt conscious that the group were slightly wary of me and that they probably (and reasonably) thought me irresponsible. They had no idea how where and when my day had begun, nor that I was on my way to Rome. They thought it surprising that I had come alone to where they had for a day trip. I waded out of the lake and having sucked my water bag dry I dug into my rucksack for the spare water I had been carrying. I drained the bottle down my throat before filling it up again from the lake. I asked the group if I could look at their map and as two of them held it I carefully took in the final stretch of the path. We waved goodbye as I left them behind me and carried on round the lake. I came to a fork and both signs forking to the left and the right read *Gt. St. Bernard Summit*. With the map in my head I took the right fork. Cursing the fat bus driver who clearly had no idea what it was like up here I continued to climb up another peak. Through my head went the words of a great friend, 'Never underestimate the power of prayer.' My feet began to go numb and I kept stumbling on the loose rocks as I climbed and prayed. Having passed the barrier of doubting my energy I eventually came to the top of the highest peak around. Looking down into another austere valley way below I could see a thin road winding its way up it. Following it with my eyes I came to what I presumed was the Hospice du Grand Saint Bernard. I was so happy. Standing next to a small cairn on a worn stone plaque that read *2950m Pointe de Drone* I laughed in disbelief and looked up at the sky. I was far above where I was meant to be but I did not care because there it was. I took photographs in both directions and one of myself having made it. I had quite a way to walk down but it seemed easy in comparison. I headed straight for the road and when I eventually hit it, I safely followed it back up to the Summit. Eventually, eleven and a half hours later having climbed a total of 3,328 metres, I arrived at six o'clock at the ancient hospice, 8,000 feet above sea level. A day that I was sure no one would ever believe.

Having been hardly able to sit up straight at dinner I was not expecting to sleep badly but I was haunted all night by the feeling of being totally alone on top of a peak looking out over hostile mountains. I woke early and was desperate to get away, out of the mountains forever. My legs felt as if they were no longer attached to my body and if I had not been so preoccupied with keeping my nerves of the day ahead under control, I am sure the pain of my left foot would have been far worse. I had bound it up yesterday morning and I paid it no further attention, not even taking pain-killers for fear they would weaken me for climbing.

As the most ancient pass through the western Alps, the history of the Col du Grand St-Bernard goes back to the Bronze Age but includes visible traces of the Roman road and records of Napoleon's march into Italy in 1800. Bernard of Menthon (923-1008), an Augustinian monk, who was canonized Saint Bernard, patron saint of the Alps, in 1681, founded the monastic hospice in 962. To this day it is run by Augustinian brothers. At dinner last night I joined a long table of 10 other guests all much older than me. I was too tired and frightened to feel hungry but I knew I must eat something. It felt like being back at school; a guest closest to one end serving everyone, several people clearing, the noise of cutlery rather than conversation, and no one particularly bothered about the person next to them. They were all Swiss or German apart from a Parisian opposite me who it turns out also spoke German. Everyone sat in silence. I tried English, French, nodding, pointing and smiling but no one was that keen to try back, however I had broken the silence and they all gabbled away in German. There was one man who intrigued me. He sat at the far end of the table with an empty place either side of him. He did not interact with anyone, ate very quickly and only ever cleared his own plate. When a man one away from him got up and accidentally scattered the cutlery, the peculiar man immediately stood bolt upright and meticulously set it all straight again. As he sat down you could see the release of tension in his body. How consuming it must be to be mad. I am aware of my own neurosis of following the same routine every night and I struggle with myself not to develop new ones such as tidying my room as if it has not been slept in before I leave. I wished I had been sitting next to this pale unusual man at the end of the table who had a mole on his cheek that looked like a dirty mark. I went into the small Baroque chapel on my way upstairs to thank God for saving me and promised once the journey was over I would never do anything so intrepid again.

Col du Grand St-Bernard - Aosta. August

Breakfast was much more sociable than the night before. I sat down next to two young men, one Turk, one South American, but they both lived in Sweden and had come here to walk six days of the Via Francigena. I chatted much more than them and whenever they did say something they would look at me without raising their heads. The Parisian then appeared and sat opposite me again. He was immaculately dressed in the same clothes as last night. Much to my pleasure the peculiar man then arrived and sat down right next to me. I eased my way into talking to him by passing the bowl of jam, saying it was too delicious not to have some. We then provided the conversation for the whole table. He was good at English although before saying a sentence he would first say it very fast under his breath in French and then repeat it to me in English. He must have been in his mid-forties but he had a child-like innocent smile and such natural charm.

Having told me he was on a peaceful retreat in the mountains I said how wonderful it was that he could find peace up here as I found them frightening. Agreeing that it was reasonable for me to find them frightening, he went on to tell several stories of people who had died in the mountains every year. Suddenly the Turk began talking as if he was trying to get his head round his thoughts. 'You must be very strong,' he said, looking at me with a lowered head, 'and it is unbelievable how far you are going as a girl alone.' His South American friend then agreed nodding his shy bowed head. Even the Parisian, who preferred to listen than to talk, managed to smile enough to say he agreed as well. It was then that I realised that it was probably confusion and surprise rather than unfriendliness that caused people to react to my situation as they did.

My sole aim today was to get to the city of Aosta in the bottom of the valley. It was a 29-kilometre descent but I knew I did not have the self-control for another night in the mountains and had I split the day I might well have lost my nerve. To begin with I followed a path so steep on one side I could not bear to look anywhere other than straight down at my feet. I wanted to sit, curl up in a ball and burst into tears but I knew this would get me no closer to flat ground. Finally, having descended very slowly, one foot in front of the other, I reached the medieval village of Saint-Rhémy-en-Bosses, where the road was wide and the land either side no longer dropped away so steeply. I passed a man sitting outside his house typing on a computer and I almost sang 'Buongiorno'. I had crossed the border of Italy at the top of the mountain and it was only this morning when I re-passed the discreet border control booth that I realised I had in fact been in Italy yesterday afternoon. As I joined an even wider road out of the village my fear subsided and spirits were lifted by a huge hello from a group of bicyclists heading uphill in the opposite direction. They waved at me and I waved my stick back smiling and smiling. I finally felt happy again.

I was heading down the Valle d'Aosta, an alpine valley in the extreme northwest corner of Italy. It is Italy's smallest region and home of the highest vineyards in Europe. I soon left the road and followed a narrow track through the woods alongside Rue Neuf, a fast flowing irrigation canal that has existed for over 600 years. It is almost 13 kilometres long and diverts the water of the Artanava River, which runs down from the Col du Grand St-Bernard to Aosta, watering an area of 424 hectares. Although some sections of the main channel have been replaced by an underground pipe, most of it is still exposed. The water was cold and I dangled my sore feet in it under the shade of the thick forest. As I got lower in the valley where orchards quenched my thirst, the temperature rose and when I reached the tourist office in Aosta they told me today had been the hottest day of their summer, 40 degrees. The very helpful woman found me a bed in a nearby convent and gave me some leaflets on the Via Francigena which is apparently well signed all the way from here to Rome. Having rung the wrong doorbell several times I finally found the buzzer for the Convento di San Giuseppe. Two black nuns opened the door just enough to see me and cowering behind it they pulled me in and nudged me towards a bare room with one table and two chairs. I took off my rucksack and struggled to talk to them or understand a word they were saying. I dug into my bag and gave the one continuously saying 'Identita' my passport. She scurried off with instructions from the other who then pointed at her watch and moved her forefinger around the face in a circle trying to give me a time, which I did not get. It would have been easier if she had written it down or held up her fingers, however, giving up, she left the room.

I had no idea what was going on but I did not mind as I was sure I would get a room. I longed to take my boots and socks off but instead sat slumped over the table waiting for something to happen. After a while the first nun to go away re-appeared with my passport and then hurried away again. Five minutes later and she was back with a tray of hot sweet lemon tea and biscuits. I had not eaten since breakfast due to terrible heartburn but now I tucked in and it was so good. The more superior watch-fingering nun then appeared with a handful of keys. I followed her to the next door down the street, up an alley, through another door, up a flight of steep concrete steps and into an attic room. Each door had a separate key including the bathroom door opposite my bedroom. The nun then left me in the absolutely baking bedroom with a small skylight that did nothing to air it.

I tried to sleep but it was too hot and shutting my eyes brought back fear of the mountains, so once my soles had recovered a little I headed out to find something to eat. Aosta is a small city that was founded in 25BC and has escaped the earthquakes and wars that other Italian towns and cities have suffered. Consequently there are many Roman ruins and medieval buildings, which still stand today. I went into the centre of town via the ruins of the Roman theatre, whose southern façade at 22 metres high still stands. Although a city, its inconvenient location at the foot of the Alps and low population give it the relaxed feel of a small town. Sitting under the loggia of the town hall looking on to Piazza Chanoux, the main square abuzz with couples and families, I ordered a Parma ham pizza in celebration of having reached Italy. I longed for a glass of red wine but I am not someone who can have just one glass and when the doctors told me excess alcohol heightens the possibility of my having fits I knew it was time to quit alcohol forever. I admit this is something I know I cannot do without help but how foolish I would look if I suffered an alcohol-induced fit, so I kept off it for the entire journey.

It is staggering what a wandering eye the Italian men have. I walk down the street feeling like I am being constantly undressed in their minds and it does not seem to matter if they are holding hands with or sitting opposite another woman, their eyes stray towards me as if they own the right to do so. This was quite a contrast to the lack of compassion of the Swiss. Switzerland was a country where everything had a price tag and nothing came for free. I did not think it as beautiful as everyone had told me. It lacked soul. I struggled to find a national identity in the character of the people, whom I found cool and ghost-like. Almost everyone flew a Swiss flag from the gable of their house in a proud manner and, unlike in France, it was as if religion were covered up. All over the French countryside there is subliminal messaging through beautiful religious statues, symbols, engravings and pietas, down country tracks, above doorways, on street corners and deep in the woods. This includes religion in everyday life. If only

Coldred to Dover, Kent

Wheat fields, Nord-Pas-de-Calais

Commonwealth war graves, Nord-Pas-de-Calais

Pilgrim stone, Apennines

Battle of Bapaume 1871 by Charles Armand-Dumaresq

Picardy

Cathédrale de Notre-Dame, Laon

Mumm & Co. Château, Champagne-Ardenne

Roman road, Champagne-Ardenne

Astronomical clock, Besançon

Ornans, Franche-Comté

La Cluse-et-Mijoux, Pontarler to Swiss Border, Franche-Comté

Lac Léman

Château de Chillon, Lac Léman

La Tsavre Mt Ferret, view back

La Tsavre Mt Ferret, view forward

Pointe de Drone, view back

Pointe de Drone, view forward

Col du Grand St Bernard

Gignod, Valle d'Aosta

Rice paddies, Piedmonte

Bard Fortress, Valle d'Aosta

Pontremoli to Aulla, Magra Valley, Tuscany

Monteriggioni entrance gate, Tuscany

Aulla to Sarzanna, Tuscany

Siena to Buonconvento, Tuscany

Buonconvento to Bagno Vignoni, Tuscany

Towards Radicofani, Tuscany

Looking back at Radicofani Tuscany

Hazel groves, Lazio

View of St Peter's, Monte Mario Park

Saint Peter's Square, Rome

more public money in the UK was spent on similar art perhaps we could restore the trust of the people and the morality of the country.

I slept badly the wrong way up in bed, enabling me to stare at the night sky through the small window in the roof. It was so hot my head lay in a sweat-drenched pillow and my nighty clung to my tired limbs.

Aosta - Nus. August

On my way out of Aosta a bicyclist weighed down with baggage drew up beside me and we spoke, he in Italian and I in English, neither of us understanding a word the other said, and for a moment we looked as though we were having a conversation. On he pedalled and I laughed a lot at the madness of it all.

I was going down the left side of the Aosta Valley with the river Dora Baltea below. The mountain ribs were steep and the excess heat was adding to the weight of my poor head. Nus was the first large town I came to and although I had not travelled very far I was desperate to sleep. I made my way towards the main road where I could see a large sign reading *HOTEL* on top of what looked like a block of flats. The hotel had a swimming pool in which I lay on my back with a view of a blue sky and the dauntingly close mountain ridge. I was longing for the day I could no longer see them and wished I could block the experience from my memory like my accident but while they loomed on the horizon the fear inside me remained. The road outside the hotel was so busy I slept with earplugs in and although I walked on dirt tracks under vines and through orchards the whole of the next day I ended up staying in Saint Vincent in a hotel equally close to the road with earplugs in.

Nus - Saint-Vincent. August

I was finding it much more difficult to settle in Italy than I expected. The ancient towns and villages seemed poor and the people uneducated. It was as if the whole area had been left behind in history, no longer the main trade route through to Switzerland and France. The countryside inside this deep V of the Aosta Valley was scattered with castles, which showed the past prosperity of a valley now covered in drooping vines. I sauntered past the defunct walls of Castello di Quart and looked out over the medieval fort of Fenis which stood proud on the other side of the valley as I made my way from Nus to Saint-Vincent. The beauty of it was overshadowed by the hydraulic dams in the base of the valley and the hideous main road, which bore its way up towards the Alps. I was struggling so much not speaking the language. I had to build up my self-confidence just to enter a restaurant and order something off the unintelligible menu while the men around stared with expressionless faces.

Having reached Saint-Vincent, I sat outside a pizzeria and ordered a salad. Half an hour later, once my empty coke can had blown down the street and I had written all my postcards, the waiter came out and realised he had forgotten about me. He returned with a half eaten bowl of salad which I ate as people passed and stared. The sun was baking hot, I was tired and sore, longing for at least a smile but none came. I went to my hotel and did as I always do: washed my clothes, showered, packed my bag and lay on the bed planning the next day. Due to the almost unbearable heat my days were much shorter than they had been. I really wanted to make it to Pont-Saint-Martin the next day if only to get further into Italy where I hoped to find pockets of happier times.

Saint-Vincent – Pont-Saint-Martin. *August*

When the morning came I switched off and went, walking 23 hilly kilometres in the baking heat. I was approaching the foot of the Aosta Valley, now alongside the banks of the river Dora Baltea. The area was far more populated and built-up but isolated castles remain on the valley ridges. I passed by the well known Renaissance Castle of Issogne and walked straight through the perfectly preserved medieval hamlet of Bard whose fortress towers above, defending from a high rock the narrow entrance of the valley. By the time I arrived in Pont-

Saint-Martin my left foot had swollen so much it was a struggle to get my boot back on after having aired my feet during lunch in a pizzeria by the Roman Bridge which is said to have been built by the Devil.

Why they had to call a pizzeria in Italy The New York pizzeria I have no idea. I sat on a rectangular balcony overlooking a busy road on the same level as the winking eyes of the endless lorry drivers. I was the last person having lunch and once the fat unshaven chef finished for the day he sat in his 'I love NY' t-shirt watching me from his legs-spread position on my right hand side. Another man, sitting outside a café on the other side of the road, kept catching my eye and blowing me kisses. Italian men certainly make up for their lack of height by their egos.

Once I had finished and paid and tried to explain that I was from Scotland not Holland, I said I was looking for somewhere to sleep. A young waiter with a face full of life who spoke the best English of any Italian I had met so far said he would drive me to the tourist office. The first thing he asked when we got in the car was, how old was I, then he asked if I was married. When I had answered both his questions he told me it was very dangerous for a young single girl to be walking alone in Italy. I smiled not too charmingly and hoped I had misunderstood him. When we arrived at the tourist office he got out of the car to walk me to the door. On realising it was closed for another half an hour he said 'we go for drive, I buy you ice cream'. I thanked him and said no. As I sat on the decking outside, he got into his car and did a several point turn whilst blowing kisses out of the open window. As he pulled onto the main road he craned his neck out of the window to continue kissing the air without looking where he was going. He clearly must have had a lot of practice at this as his car remained in a straight line.

The cheapest hotel was 2 kilometres outside of Pont-Saint-Martin but it was in the right direction for tomorrow so the pain of getting there just meant less pain tomorrow. As I walked out of the town the road got bigger, the pavement narrower and the bars on the windows thicker. I finally reached a vandalized sign which read *Hot_ _ Carla*. For the second night in a row I am the only person in the hotel but I am pleased, as goodness knows what type of people stay in these places.

For 25 euros I have got a bed with stray hairs between the sheets and a coating of matted cobwebs on the shutters. My room faces a very noisy warehouse full of machinery which never rests and between it and my window is a road heavy with fast traffic. I am lying in bed with a throbbing foot longing for a day off but not wanting to stay more than one night in these ancient, rough, grey stone towns.

I have lost the charm of the journey and I am really not enjoying it. The constant noise of the main road I sleep next to is so unsettling and, combined with the bad temper of Italians, it makes me feel on edge. Every day I see or hear from terraced houses heated arguments with male and female screeching voices. Everyday my heart-beat is also raised by the threatening dogs which are rarely chained up and come sniffing and barking up my bottom as I look straight ahead, hold my stick concealed in front of me, and walk on, pleading inwardly for them not to bite. It is a long time before I am brave enough to turn around and see if they are still creeping up behind me. Slowly the hills are getting less high and pointy and more rounded and slanted but it takes so long to leave the mountains out of view that I feel that I am actually dragging them along behind me as they slowly change shape.

Pont-Saint-Martin - Ivrea. August

The combination of drunks on the pavement and a persistent mosquito meant I had a very bad night's sleep; however, when things went wrong today they actually cheered me up. It was the prettiest day's walking I have done in Italy so far. Still on the East bank of the river Dora Baltea but the valley has opened up to the flat plains and rolling hills of the Piemonte region. I walked under hanging vines propped up on stone columns, through woods and between huge rocks. It was idyllic. I spoke to an old woman over an ivy wall. She was tidying her immaculate sloping lawn and asked where I was going. I managed to communicate to her that I was on my way to Rome from Canterbury.

She asked if I was alone and I said 'sì'. She looked up at me with eyes full of admiration and tears of concern. It warmed my insides to see what an effect my journey had on people with depth, but increasingly it also made me wallow in the emotion of it all. Having survived my time in the Alps, I knew that physically I could get to Rome. Imagining this day gave me a burning lump in my throat and made me cry tears of joy every time I thought about it.

As I was getting close to the town of Ivera where I planned to stay the night my concentration was lapsing, particularly as there were so many directions to follow over a short distance. There were a few Via Francigena markers but they were not always in the most obvious place. My left foot hurt an awful lot and I had been alternating pain-killers every two hours in baking heat so it was no surprise when I realised I was walking round the wrong side of a large lake, Lago Coniglio. My directions said *making sure you keep the lake on your left* and by now I was over halfway down the left hand side of it so continued to keep going and pick my own path to Ivera which, according to the rough map in my guide, lay just beyond and downhill from the bottom of the lake. On reaching the tip of the Lake I headed down a long steep cobbled path and much to my relief it came out on a main road heading straight into the centre. I could not see a single reference to the name of the town, which I thought was rather strange, but it did not perturb me at the time. I headed up the main road and came to a roundabout with a closed tourist information shack in the middle of it. I went into a nearby bar where there were two old men sitting at a plastic table. Of course they saw me coming and going straight up to them I laid my book on their table and pointed at the address of the Ivera tourist information and made a sign as if to say 'where?' They both looked at me and shook their heads. 'Non Ivera' one said matter-of-factly. Having no idea where I had come to, I stood looking hot and disappointed. The squatter of the two men got up and looking up from my shoulder height he rambled on. I smiled and nodded not knowing what I had agreed to but hoping he was going to help. He hobbled out of the bar beckoning me to follow. We walked up the street and he got into a pick-up. I got in to the passenger seat. Flying up the road, over speed bumps and out of the town we went. We did not even try to talk to each other but when we drove past the welcome sign into Ivera I made a very happy noise and he smiled across at me. Past the distinctive red brick Castello delle Quattro Torri, a sign off to the centre, and onto the ring road we went. I was slightly apprehensive at this stage but was quickly grounded by a big sign saying *i* for information next to a large glass building. I pointed at it and smiled. He pulled over on the edge of a roundabout and dropped me out with a big grin, a wink and a handshake.

It was only midday and the tourist office was shut until three o'clock so I went in search of the cathedral which I had read was built in the 4th century and rebuilt in the 11th and 18th century and I was intrigued to see the development of such an ancient building. As I got nearer I found myself walking up a street where almost every street-level window had a poster of the Virgin Mary in it. I thought this augured well for finding a bed. The first large door I came to had several buzzers outside and while deciding which one to press I noticed the door was on the latch so went straight in. It slammed behind me, firmly locked shut and there was no way of opening it from the inside. I turned right and walked along a huge empty corridor very amused by how on earth I would explain my situation in Italian. No one was about and my calls of 'buongiorno' got no response. I looked out of the window to my left and saw several cars in a courtyard. Knowing that they must have got in somehow, I tried to push the sash window open. To my relief it went up easily and together with my rucksack on my back, pushing my stick through first, I climbed out into the courtyard. Amazingly there was an archway open onto the street. I walked under it and back on the pavement I went on up the hill to the cathedral, prepared to pay for a hotel. This was the third church I had tried to go into today and like the other two it was shut. I stood and gazed up at the classical façade of a monstrous building. The sheer colossalness of Roman remains makes me shiver in awe of the superhuman men who built them. I wandered back through the streets passing many cafes but they were all buzzing with people and I was too intimidated to stop. When you are walking through a town, very hot, carrying a large rucksack and a shepherd's crook, as a young woman, you feel very self-conscious and a bit ridiculous so the idea of trying to mingle in with the glamorous in a bar never seems like a good idea. Before I knew it I had almost wandered all the way back to the tourist office. Seeing a sign on the street saying *salad + aqua + café 6 euros* I stopped to eat in the small empty bar. I sat at a table facing the street and ate a delicious salad. Across the road from me was a large sign saying *Hotel Eden* with an arrow below pointing at a building with a face of closed shutters. I still had nearly two hours to wait for the tourist office to open and as the hotel was next to a church I decided to risk it.

The sign on the glass door said air conditioning, which made me smile. I entered an empty reception and a hall where there was a hugely fat man watching a hazy telly. Almost certain he was the owner I put up one finger and said 'tonight'. He replied in English 'no room'. I asked if there was another hotel and getting up to go behind the reception he started tut-tutting and shaking his head at the same time. I was not going to take no for an answer just yet so I laid my stick on the floor, took off my rucksack, and sat down on the arm of the chair he had just got up from. After a lot of fumbling under the counter he pulled a key off the board and handing it to me said 'one room for you, it is double but I charge you single'. I went up to the third floor, and due to happiness I left the pain of my left foot somewhere between the lift and my cold air-conditioned double room. The bathroom, full of wrapped-up squares of soap and shampoo sachets, was so narrow I had to sit sideways on the loo with my feet in the bidet. In France and Italy no matter how small the space they always manage to squeeze a bidet in.

After 44 days almost continuously in the same pair of shorts and vest top I desperately needed to go shopping. As I went down to hand in my key I heard a throaty snore. Round the corner Mr Fat Receptionist was sprawled fast asleep on the sofa. I put my key on the counter and left.

Outside it was baking hot so first I went back to the ice cream parlour whose array of rich and varied colours had caught my eye earlier. Italian ice cream comes in every flavour imaginable unlike the American variety we eat at home, which seems to stuff all the sweetest different textured things that contain chocolate into one tub and freeze it until it is too solid to scoop. The texture of Italian ice cream makes it a complete pleasure to eat, never so cold it gives you a nose freeze and you can lick it in great loads without your tongue sticking to it. It is almost always served by a typically charmless Italian woman who stares at you with a furious face as you take your time trying to narrow down two flavours. Having pointed to the ones you want she, firmly grasping a spatula, leans into the open-top freezer, transfers her weight through her shoulder and drags the flat side of the spatula through the tub towards her, pulling it up with a pile of ice cream drooping off it. Rapidly scraping off the loose edges on the side of the tub she proceeds to wipe the ice cream on to the cone as if she is painting a ball above it. Somehow, the pile of ice cream balances on top of the cone as she repositions her full weight back over the frozen pockets for the second scoop. Then holding up your mounded cone of almost fluffy ice-cream, spatula in the other hand, she barks an amount at you. You fumble for the right change, harassed by her furious expression but salivating nonetheless. The whole process is just too good not to go through at the end of every day.

After I had eaten the ice cream, racing against the heat to try to finish it before too much dripped away on to the pavement, I got excited about the sudden thought of perking myself up with a haircut. Before I began the walk I went to our local hairdresser and said I was fed up of having half a shaved head, which was slowly growing back and please could he make it more one length so it was less obvious. Thank goodness I have short hair as in this heat I would not have coped. However it seems to have grown back long on top and still short below, not doing anything for my appearance.

I found an elegant looking hair salon up a side street and went in through the chiming door to a fragrant room of mirrors and two female hairdressers cutting the hair of two clients. One came up to me, scissors in hand, and said something. I wafted my face as if to say it is really hot and then, with the first two fingers of each hand held up to my head, mimed scissors cutting my hair. She pointed to a large cream leather armchair which I sank into and passed half an hour looking at the pictures of Italian gossip magazines. The hairdresser did a great job. We did not speak once. I sat smiling as she cut so much off my hair that it was no longer bleached blonde but I liked it. Off I went to buy some new clothes and, having tried on every type of shorts in the shop, I went away with the pair from the male model in the window. They were the only ones which had a pair of knickers sewn into the lining which saves on washing. I then bought two very cheap vest tops and headed back to my room past the still snoring hotel owner.

Ivrea - Roppolo. August

I could have gone on sleeping but having got up I went downstairs for breakfast. I found Mr Fat Receptionist in chaotic form behind a counter at the end of a hot room with several square tables all covered in dirty, blotchy, mint green tablecloths. He was standing behind a pile of washing-up in that shoulders-back stance that very fat people take up as if to give greater importance and more room to their bulging stomach. The heap of plates, saucers, cups, knives, forks, spoons and teaspoons looked more like a piece of Russian Constructivist sculpture than a sink overflowing with washing-up.

I sat down at one of the several dirty tables and watched as this unshaven man, in the hotel slippers and football strip of yesterday, laid out the contents of breakfast on a side-table. He had such a happy nature that although the whole chaotic and dirty scene put me off the food, I had to appreciate his effort. Not wanting to sound demanding I would only ask for a utensil as and when I needed it. Going to the counter he would wash it with a squirt of washing-up liquid on to a brown-stained yellow cloth under a running tap, and dry it with the damp dishcloth from over his shoulder. And so it went on as I went back and forth to the buffet and back and forth to him. No one else came to breakfast so I thought perhaps the single rooms that he said were full had in fact been building up much like the washing-up.

Having left the hotel, it took me a while to realise that the woman on the other side of the road was shouting at me. She was the proud representative of the Via Francigena in this area, not that she was capable of walking far with her jelly-like rubbing thighs. Having made a slow exit from the hotel, I was frustrated by her getting me to cross the road to her office and fill in a three-page questionnaire and then have her explain directions to me in great detail without asking whether I knew where I was going.

Today was hot, hard work, and like every other day my left foot caused me great pain. I had moved on from the banks of the Dora Baltea and was walking up and down steep wooded slopes and the mosquitoes bit and bit. I was so tired that I found myself looking up at each hill not knowing if I was going to make it to the top or not. Every step was such an effort and involved a lot of concentration. I was looking forward to lunch in Viverone; however, I only passed one bar in the main street and it was so grubby I doubted that even a fox would stop to eat there. On I went climbing up above Lake Viverone to Roppolo where I had been in contact with a woman who was having me to stay in what my guidebook called Casa Francigena. As I had not carried any food with me I was very hungry by the time I reached Roppolo so went straight past my bed for the night in search of a restaurant. I could see a castle above the village and I was sure there would be a restaurant or café on the way there. Up and up and up a steep hill I went, passing only one shut restaurant before arriving at what now looked like a very smart castle. I went straight in through the revolving glass door. To my left was a menu stand with a notice saying 'closed' so I headed right into a wooden panelled room for wine tasting. In here I found a man and woman talking in that very fast way Italians do. As I stood self-consciously dripping sweat on the stone slabs the woman could not have been more helpful and said she would drive me to a restaurant. We got into her clapped-out Polo and, after she had worked out how to reverse, headed back down the hill into the village. She dropped me out by a café which literally backs onto where I am staying. It had no sign outside but inside it was buzzing and I sat eating whatever came, loving the fact I did not have to make any choices. Afterwards I went to ring the bell of 'Casa Francigena'.

Carla answered and gave me a tour of the house. She was here for three weeks housesitting for her friends. It was her last night, I was the only person staying and she had seen no other pilgrims. This did not surprise me. There were two large rooms upstairs with three beds in each. The walls were decorated with blown-up photographs of pilgrimages on foot and bicycle. Rather obsessively these photographs went all the way down the stairs. In the study upstairs there were piles of pilgrim passports and books on a variety of different pilgrimages. The most notable feature was a large flat stone labyrinth covering most of the grass in the garden.

Carla was as nice as her character let her be. She seemed inwardly tense and unhappy which gave her a very tough exterior. I slept most of the afternoon and reappeared for a simple dinner which she had cooked. I was so nice to her and constantly saying thank-you but her smile always returned to a cold face. After dinner I did all the washing up as she absent-mindedly watched my drying and disorientated putting away. She had said 'If I cook, you clear up' but I did not think she would be so literal about it. That night I slept badly, wet with sweat and irritated by the barking dogs and reminder of each passing hour as the bells chimed close by and more followed in the distance.

Breakfast was a rush for no reason and afterwards Carla tried her best to help me find somewhere to stay between here and Vercelli. Santhià, a town not very far away, seemed the only place so I set off looking forward to a short day and lots of sleep.

Roppolo - Santhià. August

Eight days since I had met them in Orsières, resting up the track in front of me, I saw Jan and Claude. I was so pleased to see them; Jan got up and gave me an awkward hug and Claude, who is far less forthcoming, smiled up through a worn out face. They are both thin old men and hugging Jan was rather like hugging a lamppost covered in morning dew. He asked me to write down my address and telephone number for him, which I reluctantly did. We talked for a bit but, with such a sore foot, I was worried to stop too long so carried on leaving them sitting. Every day I walk far enough not to see the place I have left and although my feet and legs are not full of energy, saying 'let's go', my mind is strangely in control. It carries me on and the rest of my body follows with little choice in the matter. If I think of the distance to Rome it has much more weight than it did originally even though it is now only about 40 days away. But 40 days is the length of Lent when I usually give up bread and that always seems an awfully long time and a great achievement. I am now in it to see what happens in Rome. Deep inside it feels as though it might be the most moving day of my life. When I think about the reality of it I wonder how it is possible that walking almost every day for three months could be so moving? But there is something profound about shutting off from the usual everyday, not communicating with friends and not knowing what is in front of you to affect your mood, your thoughts, your patience, your determination and your belief.

I passed kiwi vines and apple trees as I wound my way cross-country to Santhià. On arriving I went to the church and asked one of the women doing the flowers if she spoke English. Rather than replying she touched my arm as if to say you follow me and laying down her secateurs she led me outside and round the back of the church to a buzzer which said *Parrocchia*. Out came a priest who made it obvious he wanted my pilgrim passport. I got it out and he went back inside. The woman had now left me to it and when the priest came back I mimed sleeping on my hands. He walked me down the street to a red door. Inside was Marco, a charming Italian priest with a round face behind small round glasses. Jan and Claude were standing behind him in a room with three bunk beds. Despite sharing a room, I was looking forward to the company. We all filled in forms and I saw that Jan is 62 and Claude 66. There was only one shower so after they had totally drenched the whole bathroom it was my turn. Marco, longing to help, gave us directions to a cheap restaurant on the outside of the town for lunch and also said he would book us in to a convent for tomorrow night in Vercelli.

A quarter of a carafe of red wine and Claude had a happy expression at last. We sat mainly in silence apart from their excitement over a voluptuous nude painted on the wall and expressing their longing for a massage. Jan thinks he speaks good English and French and Claude only speaks French so it would have been difficult to talk a lot; however they were totally inclusive of me in their company which was so nice. It is strange how you can bond with people without words and it almost felt like we were old friends all of a similar age. I left them and went to buy more pain-killers and anti-inflammatory gel.

That night I was asleep before they returned from dinner. However with three people in a room with no windows the temperature soon rose and we all ended up sleeping restlessly and were up and dressed by six-thirty the next morning. There was something up between Jan and Claude so I left them bickering and headed off.

Santhià - Vercelli. August

The day turned into another of cloudless blue sky and the sun shone down with baking heat. I spent the entirety of it on dry tracks along the edges of vast fields of rice saturated in water making it impossible to cut corners. Thankfully there was a breeze, which kept the mosquitoes away. I have never seen rice growing before. It is like tall lime-green grass but then the sunlight catches it and it blows yellow in the breeze. Over the rustle of the stalks you hear the constant sound of frogs plopping deep into the wet bed. It is as if they line the verge, standing to attention until the crunch of boot on dusty pebbled track gives them their cue and the echo of deep plop, plop, plop goes all the way along the verge of the field. It sounds such fun. The irrigation system is a work of art and I marvelled at it to begin with, but after 28 kilometres of a relentless view of hazy rice fields, alternating pain-killers and absolutely no shade from the baking sun I found myself shouting out aloud to try and slow down my thoughts and stop myself dropping over the edge of madness. In the last hour when I really felt like I was losing it, I plugged into my ipod, turned it up to full volume and tried to drown out the unbearable boredom of the day.

My average day's walking is always about 7 hours which when you are deep in thought passes pretty steadily; however, if you listen to music you become very conscious of every beat and therefore every second which makes getting where you are going take a very long time. Consequently I only ever listened to music towards the end of a day when it became the last resort to keep me going. Creedence Clearwater Revival's *Up Around the Bend* was the best drug I took all trip.

As I left the last of the rice fields and crossed the main road into the city of Vercelli I saw two pilgrims up ahead and quickening my pace I soon caught up with them. They were two hunched old men and I do not actually know where they had come from but they were finishing in Vercelli. I showed them the small map on the back of my book tracing the journey from Canterbury with my finger. Astounded, they immediately stopped and stared at me. One went to pick up my foot to look at the sole and then lifted my rucksack off my back to feel the weight before the other got out his camera and took a photograph. It was very funny particularly as they only spoke Italian and I could not say anything other than hello and thank you. We all shook hands and I turned right to find the convent.

I ended up walking into the drama of a fire spreading its way down the bushes of the railway line. Rapidly the streets became lined with people, blocked with fire engines, sirens blaring, and clogged with dense black clouds of smoke. I walked rapidly away from it. Finding myself near the centre of Vercelli and knowing my bed for the night was two kilometres south, I stopped for lunch in a delicious restaurant.

As I approached to have a look in the church joined to the convent I saw a very hairy armpit of a small woman inside reaching up to close the large doors. I smiled at her and she stepped forward and pointed to the next door down. I rang the buzzer and an Italian shout came down the intercom. 'Buongiorno' I called back and the door buzzed open. I went up a winding stone staircase and came out in a very long dark corridor full of clutter. At the far end I could make out a plump figure in a green t-shirt. That was Angela; a short, thigh-rubbing, chain-smoking, stout woman with a heavy dark moustache and glasses so thick I could barely see her eyes through them. Everything from writing down my details to showing me where I was on the map to reading the newspaper involved her holding the respective bits of paper so close to her face that the imprint of her nose protruded out the other side. She spoke no English and seemed to grunt rather than speak Italian.

I was shown a small cupboard jammed with bunk beds, a shower and a loo. The Convente di Billiemme is made up of two corridors at right angles to each other and both are full of bric-a-brac and furniture fit for a skip. Everything, including the handle of the bathroom tap is filthy, but thankfully the lack of lighting hides the worst of the dirt in the corridor. There was a man with only a few non-rotting teeth also looming around. Almost every time I saw him he would accidentally drop his paper packet of cigarettes and then pick them up one by one as if the longer it took him the more likely I was to go away. Angela spent most of her time squashed into a plastic chair on a narrow balcony where she chain-smoked below the drying washing. When the telephone rang she would huff and grunt and push the chair at the opposite direction to her bottom, pulling herself free and then waddle, bare feet dragging, to grunt down telephone.

Not long after I had arrived, Jan and Claude turned up. Jan gave me one of his limp wet hugs as he beamed like a child who wants to be over-involved in everyone's business. There still seems to be a frost between them. While Claude was showering Jan stood by my bottom bunk telling me how it was difficult with Claude as they move at different speeds and he was never enthusiastic. I let him complain but said nothing. I did not want to get involved in their problems. Not once did Claude complain about Jan and it was almost as if without being disloyal to Claude, Jan would have had no conversation.

At six o'clock I went to church which, stuffed full of people, was so nauseatingly hot I gave up standing. My left foot throbbed like crazy and as I sat amongst a crowd of standing figures I put my head in my hands and cried which only made me hotter. That night I woke when Jan and Claude came in from dinner. I would have liked to stay up for dinner but I needed far too much sleep and interacting with people made my head so heavy that going out for dinner was rarely an option. The bells rang so many times outside our window that at 11 o'clock we all laughed in despair.

Vercelli - Nicorvo. August

I woke at five-thirty and rushed to the loo with a dodgy tummy. Unable to sleep any more I got dressed and left. As the sun got higher in the sky the day became hotter and hotter. My tummy was so topsy-turvy it felt like I was at sea. I left Vercelli along the banks of the river Sesia and crossed the regional border from Piedmont into Lombardy dragging the rice paddies with me. My left foot caused me to walk slowly and it was not long before Jan and Claude caught up. As we entered the village of Palestro the church bells chimed to the tune of Ave Maria and it felt like a dream. Such an extraordinary situation: three people speaking different languages, heavy with luggage, sore with fatigue, meeting like old friends in a town where life is following its usual Sunday morning routine. We all went for a drink in a busy card-playing bar full of staring old men

Claude spoke to me for the first time. He told me he'd had a heart operation in July and complained of how tired he got. He also said it takes him time to get going in the morning and that the heat makes the days very hard. I was amazed. He is 66 and feels like me yet he is determined to get to Rome. It surprised me how little Jan had told me but then without Jan's unsympathetic approach I wondered if we all would have got this far together. Jan has no time for anyone else's complaints and he has certainly kept me going through his energy for each day. We all follow such a similar routine that it is as if we are one person each being encouraged to continue by the other. I have now spent two nights with them and already we are all very familiar with one another. So much so that nothing is awkward, my bra hangs to dry by their socks, their thin brown bodies wander round the bedroom in tight boxer shorts, my upset tummy is no secret and their bickering is never hidden.

That night we all stayed together again in a large peppermint green room above a garage in the very quiet village of Nicorvo. The accommodation is basic but there is a seat-less loo and a shower. The woman in the only bar in town seeing me pass her window rushed out to talk to me. I didn't understand a word she said as she took me inside and with her computer on a table we had a whole conversation through Google Translate. She then handed me the keys for the garage and told me to come back with the others, when they arrived, for dinner at seven.

Lying in bed with the window open and lizards crawling up the wall, I heard the noise of walking poles and stopped Jan and Claude as they came past. We all slept before dinner, which was a huge bowl of stodgy pasta followed by a piece of battered meat and tomatoes. The round smiley hostess hugged me when I came into the bar and throughout dinner I had to go back and forth between mouthfuls to continue a silent conversation through her computer. She gave me warmth which I desperately needed. I was finding Italy so difficult. Not speaking the language means I rely on mannerisms and facial expressions to get by and the Italians seem to be in a permanent bad mood. The bars in each town and village are always full of idle old men drinking and playing cards. They stare at me constantly but never with a smile. I am yet to pass someone who says hello or even acknowledges my presence. I feel so ostracized and vulnerable in such a poor part of the country where women seem to be kept behind closed doors and the young abandon the countryside for the big cities. I need to take a rest day but I have yet to find a place where I feel comfortable.

Nicorvo – Gropello Cairoli. August

I woke very early and lay in bed telling myself to get rid of the self-pity and dig deep for a determination to find enjoyment in what I was doing. Leaving Jan and Claude to get up I set out that morning forcing a smile on my face and a will inside me to give rather than expect warmth from others. With every person I passed I nodded my head and said 'buongiorno' and every time I did they said 'buongiorno' back. I smiled even at the grumpiest of faces and they always smiled back. Suddenly I was receiving a genuine welcome from people I had judged too quickly before. Even at the worst point of the day I did not let it rub the smile off my face and consequently I had the happiest day I have had in Italy so far.

The day began back in rice fields whose monotony was playing on my tiredness. I stopped on a bench in Mortara and ate breakfast from the bakery opposite. Shortly after the town I headed into a wood. So far the Via Francigena signs in Italy had been obvious but as I came upon a group of shabby caravans huddled in the wood there was a fork in the track and no marker sign. I sensed a nasty feeling and not wanting to hang around whilst checking my guidebook I took a guess and turned right. I went a long way down a dusty track before I thought I was far enough away to stop. Looking at the rough map I knew I had to cross a railway and a main road. I got my compass out and headed in the direction of the railway line. The track I was on came to an end at a rice field; I really did not want to go back towards the gypsy site but crossing a rice field is impossible, so instead I went to the edge which was a domed strip of brambles, thistles and nettles and I went for it. To begin with it was easy enough to step on top of them and make my way along the edge of the field. I reached the railway line, on whose other side was an equally large rice field, but this time the raised verge was taller than me in brambles, thistles and nettles. It stretched to the fast main road, which was about 25 metres away. I stood weighing up the options; the fear of gypsies was much worse in my imagination than drowning in a pile of thorns so I crossed the railway line and jumped onto the mountain of shrubbery. Into it I sank but only to thigh height. I tore up the verge and what a sight I must have looked from the main road. My rucksack, my stick and I every so often rising up above the vicious foliage only to sink back down again as the spikes grazed my arms and legs and the pollen puffed up above my head. By the time I got to the road I had a green tinge to my black clothes, grazes up and down my arms and legs and a cold prickling feeling all over every bit of bare skin. I headed down the hard shoulder to rejoin my route.

Where I should have come from there was a black girl wearing green hot pants, standing on the track. Next to her was a white plastic chair. Glancing I thought 'how peculiar' and in the way that happens when you are alone and used to talking to yourself, many thoughts rushed through my head as if all at once. I shocked myself by thinking she was a prostitute and felt guilty about pinning such a bad thought on a black woman standing in a lane but I was glad I had not walked past her. I crossed the busy road and headed on up the continuing track. There in front of me was a very similar plastic chair and a much younger black girl pacing the width of the road. She had enormous bosoms held in a lacy bra and nothing else on other than a pair of hot pants. She was humming a tune, deaf to the innocence of nature, with a pair of headphones on. It made me so sad I almost wanted to ask her to walk with me, but out of depth with the situation and frightened by it I said 'Ciao', smiled at her and walked on.

Not long after, with the noise of a car bumping up behind me, I stood on the verge and looked in through the windscreen at two faces intently focussed on the rough track. As they turned left, billowing dust behind them, my heart sank as the next signpost pointed me in exactly the same direction. I followed on and watched, as they turned right into a lonely clump of bushes amongst the flat plains of rice. As I passed where they turned I could not help myself looking. There in front of me was a young black girl bent forward clinging to the open door, shorts round her ankles, bosoms clenched by an Italian man at her rear thrusting himself back and forth into her. I carried on down the long bleak dusty track hoping never to see them again.

When I reached Tromello I entered a bar, saying hello to the glaring men outside before ordering a cup of coffee and a glass of coke. I sat inside at an empty table and took my boots off. When I looked up there was the sweetest old man grinning down at me. I recognised him from outside; he was wearing sandals, purple gingham shorts and a purple airtex. He pulled up a chair and sat down next to me. We had such an amusing time trying to have a conversation. When language is a barrier and the person you are talking to is deaf, conversation becomes charmingly simple. We held up fingers and told each other our ages: he was 73. I picked up my stick and baa-ing like a sheep I tried to explain where the horn had come from. He smiled a lot and replied in long Italian sentences none of which I understood. Once I had paid and put my boots back on he followed me onto the street. With his hand on my shoulder, telling me to wait, he went round the corner and re-appeared with his bicycle. It was painted in three strips: green, white, red, like the Italian flag. It was such a great sight with his purple outfit I made him pose for a photograph. He pushed his bike all the way to the end of the town and smiling as much as each other, we shook hands and headed in opposite directions.

I had been walking for an hour along a dusty path between the canal Cavour and a rice field when I heard the sound of a rickety bicycle behind me; peddle, peddle, squeak, squeak. I turned to let it past and there was my 73-year-old deaf friend riding his Italian flag now dressed in lime green shiny shorts and a luminous yellow vest. I quickened my pace and he wobbled beside me all the way to the next town. We hardly talked but his smile was one of complete pleasure which rubbed off on me.

When we got to the Sanctuario di Basilica Madonna della Bozzola he kept saying 'bierre, bierre', but I was not going to say yes. Bozzola is a small district north of Garlasco where there is a large church, which became a sanctuary in 1465 when a thirteen-year-old deaf-mute girl, witnessed an apparition of the Virgin. The legend tells that the young girl returned to Garlasco, no longer deaf or mute, and delivered the message of her vision. The place was made a place of sanctuary and a church was built. Ever since the Sanctuary of Madonna at Bozzola has been a place of pilgrimage and as the numbers of pilgrims increased over the years so the church was expanded to accommodate them. Together we entered the large building and made our way to a room behind the altar where the walls were lined head to foot with votive offerings. There was an intense atmosphere which I found unsettling and I swiftly headed back outside followed by the still smiling old man. He rode beside me to the end of the village and once again we shook hands and went our separate ways, waving goodbye over our shoulders. Intimate time spent in the company of strangers gave me strength to walk much further than I ever imagined in one day. I strolled on to Gropello Cairoli where, having walked 38 kilometres, I hoped to find a bed.

My soles were almost too sore to stand still on as I rang the buzzer of the door next to the church. A priest came out ranting at me in very fast Italian. I stood smiling at him and the crosser he got the more it made me smile. I said 'no parlo Italiano' and he began miming holding a telephone to his ear. I had not telephoned which I think was the reason he got so annoyed; however, he led me round the back of the church to a community centre where he left me with a bald, timid old woman who took me up to an attic room with several beds.

Realising quite how tired I was, I got into bed fully clothed and slept before showering. When I woke I had a snoop round the attic and found a room full of clothes and boxes of books. None of the clothes were up to a swap but much to my surprise I found one English book amongst the hoards of Italian ones. I wrote a note in the front of the book I had just finished and left it in place of the one I took. After a shower I took my huge appetite to find some food.

Gropello Cairoli - Pavia. August

I joined a wooded path alongside the River Ticino, a major tributary of the Po. The mosquitoes bit me so much that I ended up hugging myself to try to give them less skin to land on. When the woods stopped and Pavia was in sight the riverbank became busy with men who had an odd air about them. There were several of them, all ages, with manicured bodies, chests puffed out, broad grins and one in just a pair of y-fronts. At first I could not work out why none of them, unlike every other man I had passed in Italy, stared at me as if I was a piece of meat. The more I passed the sooner it dawned on me that they were all homosexual. There really is not much you miss out on when walking through a country.

I crossed the river through the medieval covered bridge, Ponte Coperto and entered Pavia. I then began the struggle to find some-where to sleep. I followed signs to the historic centre hoping to find the tourist office. In the buzz of the main square I went up to a security guard, swollen with muscles, and pointed at the address in my book *Ufficio Informazioni, 5 Piazza Italia, Pavia*. With several points he sent me left, right, right and left again. I followed his hand gestures and came to another square where there was a boy smoking a cigarette. Since he was the best looking person I had seen on all of the journey, I enjoyed asking him for the tourist office of which I could see no sign. He pointed directly opposite to an enormous civic building. I entered the hall of glass and pushed through the chrome turnstile towards three men in uniform. Two looked me up and down while one gave directions back to the square I had just come from. On seeing the muscular security guard again I raised my hands in the air as if to say 'I'm lost'. He pointed at the ground and said in an irascible tone 'Piazza Victoria, no Piazza Italia'. Italians really do lose their temper quickly. I decided to look round the square for myself and on finding the tourist office hidden behind scaffolding I looked back at the security guard who was still watching me and pointed at the tourist information with a big smile on my face. He shouted back 'sì, però no Piazza Italia'. He had a point but it is amazing how many Italians never do any more than the bare minimum to help.

The woman in the tourist office told me the religious accommodation only accepts male pilgrims. I then asked about hotels but the most affordable were all on the wrong side of the city for tomorrow and I never like to add unnecessary distance. I told her I would go and have a look around in the hopes of finding somewhere and if not I would be back. Round the corner from the tourist office was a large cathedral, which was closed for refurbishment but outside there were two priests deep in conversation. I went up to them and said 'Buongiorno' they both looked down on me as if I was going to say more. Grasping the opportunity I said 'Pilgrim, Via Francigena, dormioro' and then mimed laying a blanket on the floor, followed by holding my palm against my cheek with my eyes closed. When I stopped they turned to each other and continued their conversation; however, I remained hovering by their side . When they paused to look at me again I smiled back at them, willing them to give me a place to sleep. The younger of the two gave me a huge warm smile. The older one was still uninterested in me and restarted the conversation, not wanting to lose the attention of his friend. I was convinced I was getting somewhere so stood working on my tired, innocent look as they gabbled away. When the conversation ended, the older priest walked away and I quickly caught the eye of the younger one and started miming laying a sheet on the floor again. He tapped me on the shoulder and pointed to a bicycle chained against railings.

Together with his crutch and his limp we slowly walked towards the bicycle. I held the crutch as he unchained the bike and when I handed it back to him he balanced it on the handlebars. As he limped and pushed the bike, I walked by his side through the streets of Pavia not knowing where we were going. What a pair we must have looked. He had a slightly simple but sweet smile and as we walked he kept looking across and sharing it with me – once too often because the crutch slipped from the handle bars and got firmly jammed in the spokes of his front wheel. It was so funny. I tried to hold in my laughter as I pulled the crutch and he bent the spokes to release it. With the crutch back on the handlebars we continued and turned right into an alley. There in front of us was an ancient sandstone church. He pointed to it and then pointing at himself, with a simple grin, said 'My church.'

We turned left under an arch into a cobbled courtyard where he opened one of several doors into a small room that smelt of gas. The stone walls were painted pale yellow, the floor wrinkled with linoleum and all the way round the room were small wooden chairs pushed up against the walls. I beamed at him although inside I was feeling the hard floor on my hips and a sleepless night. One last time I did my laying a sheet down mime in the hopes he would give me a blanket. Taking me out across the courtyard he opened another door and there in a long corridor was a mattress propped up against the wall. I dragged it back to my bedroom while he unlocked a padlock on a stable style door; inside was a hole in the floor and a sink. I was so grateful I thanked him in English and he left with an even bigger grin on his face. Slightly worried by the smell of gas, I stood on a chair and turned off the only pipe I could find with a tap on it and just hoped everything would be all right.

I went to have a look in the adjoining Basilica di San Michele Maggiore. It dates from the 11th and 12th century and although now cramped by the small streets of the city it is an imposing Romanesque building. Inside its dark interior there are the most wonderful medieval carvings. The capitals all the way along the nave depict biblical scenes and underneath the raised altar in the crypt are many more naïve carved capitals and tympanums with angels, winged dragons, foliage and figures. Tired and hungry I went in search of some food and returned to eat it on my mattress on the floor.

I slept so well that when my alarm woke me I longed to go back into a deep sleep but this was not the luxury bedroom I was hoping to find for a day off, so I got up telling myself that very soon I would be able to sleep for a whole day.

Pavia – Santa Cristina. August

The archway that the kind simple priest had led me under yesterday had two gates bolted shut across it at six-thirty this morning and every shutter above the arch was closed. Digging an apple out of my rucksack I slowly ate it as I paced the courtyard and thought about what to do. Time began to pass and it was not long before I heard the creek of shutters opening. 'Buongiorno' I shouted looking up to see who was awake. The shutters, not even open enough to see me, were quickly pulled to again. 'Buongiorno, buongiorno, buongiorno' I continued to shout, lifting my arms in the air and waving. Ever so slowly one of the two shutters began to creak open, a small gap was being created and an old woman's head with a mouth empty of teeth poked out just enough to get a look at me. I jumped and patted my chest and pointed at the arch out of view beneath her as I made an action of unlocking. With an expressionless face she pulled the half open shutter shut. I pulled on my bag, sure she was coming to help me. Hunched over, in a long blue nighty, fluffy slippers and bosoms surprisingly un-saggy for her age, the old woman appeared and unlocking the gate wished me 'buon viaggio' as I was let loose into the street. I hung my head back on my rucksack and smiled a big smile at the totally blue sky.

I continue to have to wear a tubi-grip and alternate ibuprofen and paracetamol every two hours to keep the pain of my left foot as dull as possible; however, today it hurt much more than ever. With only an apple inside me the ibuprofen soon took its toll on my tummy. Fortunately out of the rice fields and into high maze made going to the loo a lot easier. Apart from having to negotiate crossing the busy ring road out of Pavia, I spent most of the morning on country tracks and quiet roads. Heading against the traffic I passed a man on a bicycle who shouted at me aggressively as he pointed at the other side of the road. Had I understood I probably would have cried but instead it made me laugh a lot. Italians so rarely walk they probably do not know the safest way to go about it. Shortly after heading up towards Belgioioso, I passed a very old bicyclist, who waved with such enthusiasm I don't know how he stayed on his bike, which did an amazing half figure of eight veering to the other side of the road.

I am heading towards the Po river in the south of Lombardy; it is a rough area and the small villages, full of leering drunks, have few facilities. I made it to Santa Cristina in time for lunch and, desperate for some food, I went into the only restaurant before trying to find a bed. I am getting used to eating in empty restaurants where they do not even bother to turn the lights on. Menu of the day for 6 euros gets you pretty full and there is wine included if you are allowed and a large bottle of fizzy water if not. After each of three courses I had to rush to crouch over the smelly hole in the floor as what I ate came straight out the other end. I left the restaurant, feeling emptier than I was when I went in, and went to knock on the priest's door.

Round the back of the church was a community centre set-up similar to the one I had come across two days ago. It seems Italian village churches run a hang-out for energetic children and grown-ups who have lost their direction in life. I walked into the bare room and was welcomed straight away by several smiling faces stuck in their chairs and one lopsided man who I doubt would have made much sense even if I had have spoke Italian. He led me up a concrete staircase into a room, which had a bed with springs so big I could probably bounce and touch the cobwebs dangling from the very high ceiling. Then with that heavy limp lopsided people have, he took me down the corridor to a large room full of mattresses. He said something to me, of which I did not understand a word, before thumping his way back downstairs.

The place is so filthy I do not even want to put my rucksack down. I opted for the single room and dragged the cleanest of the mattresses through from the large dorm. I flung open the window onto a playground below and went to find the bathroom. It was filthy and every plug was blocked with hair. The sink overflowed before it drained and after showering I ended up standing in a puddle of my own dirt. Despite the cobwebs, dusty crunchy beetles on their backs and dried brown rims on the floor, I felt amazingly clean having washed for the first time in two days. I lay on the stained mattress as the smell of cigarettes wafted through my window and the ping-pong ball bounced off either end of the table.

My foot was too sore for me to sleep so I went to the chemist I had passed on the way into town. It was an old-fashioned chemist and behind the counter sat a man on a high stool wearing glasses on a string. Behind him were rows of tablets and bottles lined up in glass cabinets. In the corner was a small glass refrigerator with some particularly medicinal looking substance in it. I smiled at him as much as I possibly could and he loved it. I then acted out my journey, my sore feet, and my search for arnica – pills, not cream. The more my story developed the more over-excited he got. By the time it came to paying he was bubbling over with excitement and trying to give me more change than I had paid him in the first place. As I turned to give him one final smile before the door bell pinged behind me he hopped up and down on his stool as if it were piping hot saying 'bellisima, bellisima, bellisima' through a broad grin. This cheered me up a lot since on the rare occasions in Italy when I came across old men either behind a counter or flanked by a sturdy wife, I did enjoy getting them into a mushy state.

Back at the community centre I heard people in the big dorm so went to say hello. They were a Dutch couple, Evert and Marinka, who had walked from the Netherlands and were also heading to Rome. I could not get over how brown they were but I guess I am a similar colour too. They look so weathered but very fit and they could not have been happier. They are probably about 50 but seem to have an ease about them, which makes them seem much younger. We all discussed tomorrow when we need to get a boat across the river Po and they kindly suggested we all walk together. They would have suggested we ate together but I said I must sleep. I did not go into it but it is hard for people to understand how much sleep I need. I would love to stay up for dinner or join the simple people downstairs who practically begged for me to drink Lemoncello with them but my head is in control and it is not going to let me.

As I was going to my room I met the priest in the corridor. Thankfully a delicious-smelling woman who spoke good English accompanied him. We all sat in the dorm, each telling him, through the woman, a bit about our journey before asking if he would book the boat across the Po tomorrow. Although the pilot, Danilo, has an unreliable reputation, the priest assured us that the boat was booked for two-thirty tomorrow afternoon.

Last night was terrible. The mosquitoes went mad for me. I got dizzy with a shoe in my hand trying to kill every single one before getting back into bed. It was hot but I did not dare open the window. My legs, back, shoulders and arms were lumpy, bumpy all over. The bites began to itch so much I covered as many of them as I could reach with hydrocortisone. Thinking they might actually be bed bugs, I laid my sleeping bag flat on the bed and wrapped myself like a sausage roll in a sheet I found in the cupboard. But still the incessant buzzing filled the dark room and they now bit my cheeks, my ears and the back of my neck. I turned on the light and lay very still, snatching in the air every time their angular figures made a b-line towards me. With so much wriggling my big toe had escaped the confines of the sheet and they bit it as soon as it was free. It was midnight, my body was one big hot itchy ball and I could not imagine ever falling asleep.

I got up and took off my nighty, zipped up my sleeping bag, got into it, and pulling the draw string with my teeth so it was tight round my neck I built up the most unbearable furnace in the down bag. The last time I looked at my watch it was 2:41am and I woke at 5:30am with a mosquito buzzing in my ear. At 6.15 I gave in and slowly, heavily, full of tiredness I got up.

Santa Cristina - Calendasco. September

I met the Dutch couple downstairs and we walked out at seven o'clock under a low hung grey sky. We had hardly made it out of the village before the most enormous raindrops began to fall. It was not long before it seemed as if the gaps between the drops had closed and someone had opened the canal floodgate and water was gushing, gushing, gushing down on us. Standing under a tree we pulled on our waterproof coats and bag covers. The rain was so heavy that the tree offered little shelter, so we carried on. To begin with it was amusing but soon the sky became very dark and the rumble of thunder was too loud to talk over. Suddenly we were in the throes of a thunderstorm and the lightning struck so close it forced us to blink. There was no gap now between the clattering rumble of thunder and the lightning, which forked down from directly above. It was absolutely terrifying. Marinka and Evert turned to me and said 'You're from the country, what do we do?' I ashamedly had no idea but seeing the fear in their eyes I made a decision and said we must get to the town in the distance as quickly as possible. We were in the middle of fields on an open track with electricity wires strung above us. The town was close enough to get to but far enough to risk our lives getting there. It was far less frightening than it would have been alone and I knew I had to stay strong to give them hope. We ran as fast as we could, rucksacks swaying from side to side as our feet splashed along the chalk path. Each time the lightening struck and the reflection bounced off the water at our feet I prayed with all my heart it would not hit us.

We made it to the overhang of the first building in the village and pulling off our bags, out of breath, we were silent with shock but safe. We stood watching the clouds billow their way in the opposite direction, as the rumble became fainter and the rain slowly stopped. I wrung out my socks and we continued towards a blue patch of sky and more rice fields.

Mainly following tracks we walked in a row with me sandwiched in the middle. They insisted on buying both rounds of coffee as we warmed up in a bar. I ate two soggy croissants I had been carrying and by lunchtime I had no more food. We stopped on a park bench, the sun was now out and we aired our feet. They produced two bread rolls and a can of swordfish, which they insisted on sharing. I was so hungry it did not take much persuading. All day they spoke in English even to each other and always made time for me. Whether it was queuing to post a parcel or having to stop for coffee in the afternoon to try and get some energy, they always waited and never complained. They were so in love and so nice to each other I felt as if I was with Muma and Papa whose wedding anniversary it was today.

The best part of the day was the wind blowing into one's face as we crossed the river Po in Danilo's boat *Taxi*. When we mounted the opposite shore, now in Emilia-Romagna, Danilo led us to his house where there was a group of his friends outside, sitting back in chairs drinking homemade wine. There were two old men, an old woman and a young man with the most beautiful long dark eyelashes. We three sat on a bench and were given coffee and coke, while the others had wine; we had delicious apricot tart which I ate most of. We stayed for over an hour and I moved from seat to seat trying to talk to the Italians, which amused everyone. The Dutch have such good manners that it stops them invading other people's space or searching for the opportunity of conversation when it isn't necessary. I was so used to being alone that talking to new people was too much fun not to try. What's more when we said goodbye I got a garlicky kiss off the oldest of the men.

At the next town we came to, Calendasco, we decided to stop for the night. It was a shabby place and the countryside around it was ugly. Huge flat furrowed fields with the largest lumps of dry cracked mud I have ever seen. The whole area was dusty with heat as it stretched out parallel to large pylons. We walked round the corner of a building, which said 'Ospitallia', and there were several very black men lounging on sofas under the shade of an overhanging veranda. It was too late to turn around by the time they had seen us, so we inquisitively kept going to the next building out of which came Marion's broad Birmingham 'welcome'. She was a plump, greasy black-haired woman ready to welcome whoever needed a roof. With an enthusiastic smile of yellow-stained teeth nothing was too much for Marion and she showed us up to a dormitory of several beds.

As the others showered and changed I went to make friends. Marion having married an Italian had lived in Italy for years. She ran the place with her son, daughter and daughter's boyfriend. The very black people were forty male Ghanaian refugees whom she had accepted from Tripoli but she was struggling to get their papers. Consequently she has found herself feeding and housing 40 people with no money and no work permit. Marion's enormous heart has led her down a path that the locals resent her for.

After I had washed and slept I went downstairs to join Marinka and Evert but first I sat with one or two of the refugees. As I began to ask a few of them about their situation more of them came to hover around listening in with their big white eyes glaring at me. They were lazy with the heat and lacked motivation but who could blame them. Most had young families back home and when I asked why they chose to leave they said they were in search of greener pastures. However all of them have a loyalty to their country and want to return. They are here to earn money but until they get their papers that is impossible. Marion is feeding them, housing them and teaching them at the expense of her local reputation. No one comes to eat at her restaurant any more and the Italian government's promise of a grant is yet to materialise and so she is caught between a responsibility and an expensive situation as well as the unknown of what boredom will bring out of their characters. What a dire situation they are in and what a moral dilemma Marion has brought upon herself.

Not knowing a thing about their culture makes it very difficult to read them. They have a frightening stare, which goes straight through you. As I spoke with them it was very quickly brought to my attention that one man in particular did not have a wife and would very much like one. For the rest of the evening as I ate dinner outside with Marinka and Evert, this man did not take his eyes off me. Although obscured by a post he was always looking. I was relieved to be sleeping in a dorm with Marinka and Evert, them in their underwear, sharing a double bed, and me in a camp bed by their side. How close we had got in one day.

Walking with other people makes such a nice change from my own company but it wears my head out. Mentally I am still so unfit and by being amongst company I really notice how much more tired I get and as I get tired my memory and words get in a muddle, which makes me feel so stupid. By dinner last night I was so worn out I could not follow the conversation. With the background noise it takes so much concentration and I had no energy to try. Instead I just agreed with whatever they were saying and eventually excused myself and went to bed. I am conscious of the contrast between how fine I look to how unwell I am in the head. It is different to being conventionally tired: your stamina rapidly runs out and takes your ability to process information with it and you suddenly know that you have to go away and close your eyes. It is as if I am constantly being told what not to do and always having the day cut short by sleep. When I get tired amongst company I can feel myself slipping down a simple slope and I get the urge to remove myself before anyone notices. The whole situation makes me so unhappy but I try not to dwell on it. Time will tell if I get better and at least during a bit of that time I should have walked to Rome.

Calendasco - Montale. September

The next day I had such a heavy head and was so incredibly tired that when I stepped it felt as if the ground was disappearing from beneath me and then catching me just before I fell. When we reached the centre of Piacenza midmorning I kissed Marinka and Evert goodbye and said I had to stop. I went to the tourist office and found a lazy, difficult woman who told me there was a conference going on and all the accommodation in the centre of town was full. She then handed me a list of names, addresses and telephone numbers. I was very sensitive to her cold manner and said 'I do not want to be difficult but as you know the city please can you tell me the options closest to the centre and then as I don't speak Italian...' 'I know you don't speak Italian' she butted in with a sharp tone. '...Perhaps you could call and see if there is space?'

She called three places on the outskirts of town which were all full. Reluctant to let her run out of patience, I looked on the map for a place on my route out of Piacenza and pointed at a B&B. They had one space but I had to arrive within an hour. She gave me a map that was too big to hold out in the street and told me to take the third turning on the right and keep going. After half an hour I stopped a woman in the street and as I fumbled around finding the bit of paper with the address on it I tried to get my words out. Having found the bit of paper I looked down at her and smiling up at me she tapped her ear to tell me she was stone deaf. I went into the nearby supermarket and as I paid for a basket of food I asked the checkout girl for directions. She pointed straight down the road I was on. I walked for another half an hour past car salerooms, mobile phone shops and estate agents, none of which had a number plaque on them. I went into an estate agent but the girl behind the desk did not recognise the address of the B&B and instead confirmed I was on the right road. Having walked for over an hour I knew I must have passed the B&B but reluctant to turn back I carried on down the pavement of a now very busy main road. When I came upon a church that was wedged between two derelict buildings with their windows smashed in and graffiti scrawled along the walls, I went in and prayed my daily rosary right up at the front as my feet throbbed in pain. Back outside I rang the intercom by the Parrocchia door. A woman let me in and pointed at the priest. He got up and recognising my needs he gave me a key and handed me a photocopied road map, which had a cross marked further down the main road I was on and the number 189 written by the side. I thanked them and left clutching the key and cheered up by the sheer good fortune of it all.

Three kilometres later I let myself into an empty stone building. On the ground floor there was a chapel and a dark kitchen and up a narrow stone staircase I came to a landing with a dorm and a bathroom. Up one more floor was a wooden-beamed room with two beds and a bathroom. There was no sign of anyone so I settled for the smaller room. I showered, turned the mattress over, ate lunch and then slept as well as I could. Behind my red metal headrest there was a stone wall of the bell tower. I am just slightly below the bell and every quarter I am given such a fright by the very loud doing, doing, doing, of the bell as the tower shudders and creaks under its weight. On the hour the bell rings forty times before it is left to drown out its own noise. Sadly this is no place for a day off.

Already I was missing the company of the Dutch couple. The nicer the people are the harder it makes it to find yourself alone again. I was jealous of their companionship and shared experience but I knew I must settle back into the luxury of losing myself deep in my own thoughts. I have now spent fifty-three days trying to work out what will challenge me the most while giving me a profession as well as a purpose for my existence. Being part of a spoilt generation with so much choice and so many opportunities makes it hard to identify a path to live along and a steady foundation to build on. When things get tough it is easy to change tack and try something new without guilt or feeling one has failed. I went to five different schools, one university and have had six different jobs in the space of 28 years. I desperately need to find a purpose in life and give it all I have got.

I believe inner happiness comes by remaining on one path and once the hard part has been conquered you reach a blissfully rewarding stage that you did not know was ahead of you. Trying to identify that path is difficult. This pilgrimage is essentially a very selfish time for me to look at where I have gone wrong in the past and work out what it was I kept running away from. I knew the only way I could achieve this was by being alone which is why from the very beginning I was not afraid, as it was time for me to face my own thoughts. The physical challenge of the journey is a way of validating my theory that unknown happiness comes from sticking on the same path. Whatever it takes I must get to Rome.

Montale – Fiorenzuola d'Arda. September

I ate a tub of yogurt in the empty kitchen listening to the early morning traffic and working out a cross-country route to Fiorenzuola d'Arda. I left along the busy main road and traversed the first field I came to into the safety of the countryside. A small dot of a milky orange sun soared its way up the hazy dawn sky as I crossed field after field of tomatoes. The smell was so strong it put me off wanting to taste one. I entered a wood knowing that when I came to the river I must follow its banks. The area was so dry the river-bed was indistinguishable and I found myself heading far too far south on a network of trails through the trees. I felt frustrated by the thought of heading back in search of the river so instead I kept going towards a town I could see in the distance.

A very helpful woman sitting alone in a bar talked me through directions to rejoin my route, which somehow I had managed to veer ten kilometres away from. I drank a cup of coffee, secretly hoping she would finish her croissant and offer to drive me but she didn't. If I had decent maps I would not get lost half as much as I do; however, the people I meet when I am lost are always the nicest and therefore early on I convinced myself to pursue the journey without spending money on maps.

Seven hours later with very sore feet I had eventually made it to Fiorenzuola d'Arda. I stopped in the first ice cream shop I saw and whilst filling up on cold, sweet ice cream I decided, as tomorrow was Sunday, I would take the much shorter main road route to Fidenza. Whatever the town was like I promised myself I would take a day off. This gave me something to look forward to as I went in search of a bed.

There was a vast wooden arched door next to the church and it had a choice of several names on the intercom. I randomly pressed one and shortly after the brass letterbox squeaked open and out peered two wrinkled blue eyes. 'Solo?' the peeper said. 'Sì,' I beamed. The door opened a crack and a miniature hunchback wearing huge shiny black shoes, which I guess had to be a certain size for him to balance upright, motioned for me to come in. On the other side of the door was a high-ceilinged stone entrance hall. He pointed at the one wooden chair up against the wall. I removed my bag and sat down in the sunken floral seat as he shuffled into a room by my side and started pounding away on a typewriter, continuing with whatever it was that I had interrupted. Finishing, he tore the bit of paper off the reel and bent over, drooping nipples visible through his faded t-shirt, he shuffled back past me and went upstairs. I sat listening to what sounded like him brushing his teeth. He came back down and looking at me, worn out on the chair, said 'Identité'. With my passport ready in my hand I followed him into a room with a large photocopier. Pressing down the lid as if it had a spring in it I caught sight of his enormous go gadget watch and raised my arm to point at it. He leapt out of his skin and pulled his arm away at great speed. I pointed at my watch and then back at his, and giving it a thumbs-up I tried to calm his nerves and convey that that was all I had in mind. He was so shaken up I gave him space and went back to sit in the hall.

With the photocopy complete he handed me my passport and headed back into his office. Pulling out a drawer in his desk he proceeded to pick out 22 keys all with identical purple tags. As he did it he inspected each one individually and then, picking them all up at once, he led me out through a back passage, pointing with his elbow as I opened the doors. Out of the building and up a back alley we came to a doorstep on which he carefully piled all the keys. Picking up one with no apparent method in his choice he unlocked the door and I walked in completely baffled. He pointed straight up the stairs and directed me to a room on the left. I turned to offer him money but he refused and that was the last I saw of him.

After flooding the bathroom because of a blocked shower plug I slept soundly for three hours. I woke very hungry and went in search of a supermarket. Standing outside a bar full of glaring fat old men slumped into plastic chairs I said my standard introductory sentence,

'No parlo Italiano' followed by a questioning 'super-market?' They all continued staring and not one of their expressions changed. One man stepped forth, looked me up and down and said 'Come, come.' Slightly worried that he was taking me to his car I followed him down the street. The first junction we came to he pointed down and said 'Supermercato'. I had built up an appetite in the tomato fields for mozzarella and combining it with local Parma ham I returned to the empty house and ate in a kitchen which appeared to be lived in, but no one was around. I slept undisturbed looking forward to a day off.

Fiorenzuola d'Arda – Fidenza. September

At seven o'clock the next morning, much to my surprise, the church doors were open. It was a vast building and I climbed the steps to have a look inside. As I entered Mass was just beginning. This church, a collegiate, has three naves, so hidden by an enormous cylindrical stone pillar, I was able to sit in a side aisle, where my underdressed appearance went unnoticed. In Italy every Mass I have been to, no matter what time of day, is always stuffed full of people and more often than not families. The churches, both big and small, are flamboyantly decorated with swirling plasterwork, gold leaf and ceilings covered in pastel frescoes. So rich in ornament are they that you get a strong sense of celebration and for children gazing up at the ceiling it must make them feel as if they are sitting inside a huge, colourful storybook.

Having sat for an hour I had lost the early morning energy for the day ahead and plodded my way out of town with heavy legs along an increasingly busy road. It was the first time I had walked along an extremely busy main road and I was not going to do it again. Even on Sunday the traffic was relentless. Several tooting horns got me smiling but otherwise I feared for my life. It took such concentration not to drift off into thought that it suddenly became clear why I got lost quite so often. The cars drove close to the verge and the lorries created such a gush of wind I had to stand still as they passed to avoid losing my balance. The cars overtaking on the other side of the road gave me the biggest fright of all. I no longer have peripheral vision on my right hand side and the shock of a car suddenly appearing from close behind shook me with terror of being run flat in seconds. I hated every minute of the three hours it took to get to Fidenza. Not only is it filthy walking along the main road but there is also no opportunity to go to the loo. Absolutely bursting I went into the first café I came to.

On my way in to the town I was pleased to find the tourist office open. The man behind the counter had wonderful long, dark eyelashes and I found myself unintentionally flirting with him. We talked at length about the Via Francigena, where I should stay and how little there was to do in the town. When I came to leave he clung onto the conversation and I felt unfair turning off the heat and leaving him mid-sentence to go find the cheap room he had booked me into.

I buzzed the buzzer of a grim brown building up a dead end street. There was no answer so I buzzed again. From the top row of plastic shutters an old woman stuck her head out, put her fingers in her ears and shouted something at me. I think I save myself a lot of criticism by not speaking Italian. A shaven-headed man with a hoop ear-ring and a tight t-shirt opened the door and shook my hand, speaking good English with an East London accent. He took me upstairs to a simple room and clean communal bathroom and asked me to pay cash then and there since I probably would not see him again. I was given a swipe card to let myself in and out. It was black with a white skull and crossbones on it and for once I felt as if I fitted in quite well with my short spikey hair and traveller image. Whenever there is a crucifix in a bedroom I don't feel frightened and thankfully here there was one above the door.

Fidenza is a charming medieval town; the main square is compact but full of life, a place where people sit and chew the fat, where families walk and old people ride bicycles. A large cathedral built in the 12th century cramps the small streets. Legend has it that it was built on the site where San Donnino, beheaded for his Christian belief on the banks of the River Stirone outside Fidenza, miraculously placed his severed head. The importance of this Saint as protector of travellers and pilgrims, and the fact that his remains are kept in an urn under the altar, made this cathedral a key place for people on their way to Rome. So much so that on the outside wall there is one of the first ever road signs to Rome, a statue of the apostle Saint Peter, pointing, who holds in his left hand an inscription reading *I show you the way to Rome*. The three doors of the main façade have wonderful medieval stone carvings of various animals and bas-reliefs depicting the story of San Donnino.

During the 43 hours I was in Fidenza I spent 37 in my room, mostly sleeping and, if not, watching my washing dry as I kept my feet off the ground. It was a little lonely at the same time as being wonderful: wonderful for the soles of my feet that tingle with numbness; for the bridge of my left foot which gives me permanent pain; for my head which was so heavy on the right hand side that it was weighing down the lid of my eye. By the time it came to leaving again, I was ready to go although a large part of me was dreading the forthcoming mountain pass in the Apennines, even though at 1041 metres it was nowhere near as high as the Col du Grand St-Bernard.

On my day off I had tried to make my bag lighter. I made a small pile of things I could do without and a small pile of things I could send home. It was Muma's birthday and I had bought her a pair of cosy pyjamas, the kind she likes that warm the whole body. I had finished another diary and putting it all in a bag I went to find a box. Behind the counter in a clothes shop I spied one that the woman gladly gave me. I then went to the post office to wrap it up and send it but the cashier for some reason said I needed to come back at nine o'clock the next morning. Reluctantly I left, not wanting to leave so late tomorrow but also knowing I could not carry a large cardboard box with me. I went into a nearby cafe and in despair I explained my problem as best I could to the woman behind the bar. Leaving her with an open box full of good things and a certain amount of English and Swiss change within it, I handed her 40 euros and wrote an address for the box. I just prayed she had a Catholic conscience and that there was enough change for her left over to ensure she posted it.

Fidenza - Sivizzano. September

I was woken by my alarm at six-thirty. It was dark and pouring with rain outside. I had bought some sort of pink creamy ball from the bakery yesterday. A woman in the queue with very short hair, dressed like a scout, was chatting me up. She spoke good English so I asked her to suggest something that would keep until the morning. The sweet smell of the pink creamy ball was almost too tempting to sleep next to all night so when I was woken from a deep sleep I wasn't too disappointed as now I could finally eat it. It kick-started my day and away and into the rolling foothills of the Apennines I went.

The sky was evil and threatening all day but it looked worse than it was and the rain soon stopped. To begin with my foot hurt so much I asked myself if I wanted to go home but faced with the question I said no. I really would love to go home but I also hated the thought of not getting to the end. I now no longer believed I was going to get there but while I was still able to put one foot in front of the other I would keep going. With this thought I did not dare stop all morning, during which I was joined by a white retriever. Company, as I nicknamed him, was with me for over an hour and would walk just in front of me as if leading the way. If I slowed up he would stop and stare at me and once I was close enough he would spring into a walk again. He barked violently to scare off any other stray dogs and although I was slightly worried he might suddenly turn on me I was so happy to have Company. Eventually we met a man walking a dog. My white companion went up to him and the man took hold of his collar and read his name-tag. Worried that the man would want me to take responsibility for returning the dog, I walked straight on and paid him no attention, feeling pretty guilty and missing my companion. I stopped in a bar in Medesano for coffee and a croissant that tasted as if the butter was off. An old man chatted me up and when he started telling me how lonely he was I got an urge to carry on to the next town.

The countryside was gloomy, rising and dropping steeply and decorated with huge pylons. The ground was so muddy my feet picked it up and suffered under the extra weight. I reached the bottom of a valley and crossed a long bridge over a thirsty river into Fornovo di Taro. I went into a supermarket to buy bread rolls and canned fish, something I had developed a taste for after meeting the Dutch couple. As I pointed at a roll the old baker amused himself by asking me rather too many times whether I liked it hard or soft. I ate on a dreary bench in an empty car park facing the drop-outs loitering outside the supermarket and then headed in search of the tourist office.

It didn't open until four o'clock and it was only two so I kept going into the dismal centre and sat at a high chair by the bar drinking coffee. The burly owner who fancied himself fell for my body language which suggested that I was looking for conversation. I told him I was looking for a bed and he said I could share his but he also had a wife. He didn't speak English so everything I asked or he said had to be interpreted by the jealous bar lady. I asked him to call the church in a village eight kilometres further on to see if I could spend the night there. He was too much of a joker for me to know if he was being sincere or not but he said they had a bed for me. The woman gave me a bill for the coffee; I paid, and as she went to put the change in the till, the man made her give it to him and he gave it back to me. I left and not having had many for a few hours I took an ibuprofen and a paracetamol at the same time. Absentmindedly I had not read the altitude scale and was surprised to discover that the entire eight kilometres into the Sporzana Valley were uphill.

Forty-two kilometres later, the furthest I have ever in my life walked in one day, I arrived in the tiny village of Sivizzano and found my way to a charming courtyard round the back of the church. An old woman let me in through iron gates under an arch and led me into a long cellar with three camp beds. Her husband appeared, a jolly man who spoke a few words of English. They were so excited to see me that perhaps they had not seen any newcomers for a while. I had no food but the old man said he would drive me to a nearby shop. Having taken my telephone out, I left my rucksack in the stone vaulted cellar and went to buy dinner. Muma and Papa knew I was nervous about heading into more mountains and had asked me to send them a text message each night to tell them I was safe. I was in an area with no reception but I knew somehow I must get a message to them. Clutching my telephone I explained my problem to the old man who happily drove me back down the valley until the bars appeared. For him it was an opportunity to wave at everyone we passed and show off the stranger in his car.

I showered and lying in bed completely worn out I ate a whole packet of chocolate biscuits. If I did not have to stop for night-time I think I would have been happier continuing up, up and up just to get the mountains over and done with in one day but this was not an option. I had gone so far today it stopped nerves about the next two days interrupting my sleep and I slept, wrapped up in rugs, alone and unafraid in the cellar of an ancient Benedictine monastery.

Sivizzano - Berceto. September

I left Sivizzano as it was just beginning to get light and spent a long and strenuous morning climbing up and up and up the Apennine Mountains on narrow paths and forest tracks. It was very pretty and, although hard work, I felt so fit and my left foot was far less sore going up a steep gradient. I passed a stone carving of a pilgrim who aptly had a very grumpy expression. I was sure he had come from Canterbury too.

Unlike the Alps, which are so high that they have no life at the top of them, the Apennines are beautiful and unthreatening. The unspoilt countryside and lush sloping fields of grass are tinged with a deep blue and the trees in the forests are so tall that they form a canopy above you with little vegetation underneath, making it easy to see through. The mountains, although high at the peak, push their way up plateaux, forming valleys at varying levels. Villages and towns lie in each valley and never being faced with an uninhabited view gave me such comfort.

Overlooking the Baganza valley I passed through the paved stone streets of the ancient village of Casola which, hidden away in the mountains, has been well preserved. It is a small place but it was an important town on the main historic route through the Apennines, for soldiers, traders and pilgrims on their way to the sea and Rome. The iconic central bell tower is the only surviving part of its 15th century castle; however, its rich past is evident in the still standing Palazzo Lombardelli, a Renaissance palace built in 1544. I stopped in a bar for my morning energy boost of coke and coffee and with restored strength in my legs pushed on up the mountain to find a larger town.

I arrived in Bercetto by one o'clock and there in the small historic centre were Marinka and Evert sitting outside a hotel drinking coffee. I was so pleased to see them. They have been here for two days and were as happy as when I had left them. I went into the bar and asked about food. The woman pointed down a corridor into the back of the building and before I could turn around I found myself crashing into a civilised dining room. I dug a wrinkled t-shirt out of my rucksack and sat hot and self-conscious in a room full of old people dressed as if they were being taken out to lunch and silent couples that were now content to have me to watch. The menu was so expensive I chose one first course and ate it slowly enough to fill me up.

I went to the small main square at one side of which is the enormous Romanesque cathedral of San Moderanno. I was hoping to find a bed but the cathedral was shut and there was no obvious Parrocchia buzzer or house nearby so I went down a narrow street to the tourist office. It was also closed and did not open again until four, so I returned to the main square where I sat for two hours eating ice cream and watching people. I did not mind the wait, as I was so happy to be over half way up the mountains and safe.

Leaving my rucksack leaning up against a trough of flowers, doubting anyone would cut through the smell of dried sweat and pinch it, I went into the tourist office. An unhelpful anorexic woman told me I needed to find the priest, Don Giovanni, and he would let me into the community centre where there were beds for pilgrims. I asked her where to find him and she replied 'Near the duomo'. I knocked and knocked on a door that I found round the back of the Cathedral but there was no answer, so I went back to sit in the main square with my eyes peeled for a priest. It was not long before I spotted two nuns who tried to avoid my gaze as I rushed towards them. As I struggled with Italian one of them suddenly pointed and said 'Don Giovanni'; I turned round to see a man dressed in lay clothes and wondered how on earth I would have found him. He was slightly alarmed by my enthusiasm for hearing his name and sent me back, with a pointed arm, to sit by my bag while he chatted with the nuns.

Italians just love to stand around talking. They never seem to be saying anything particularly important and actually I think they are just putting off what they have to do. On the way to the community centre Don Giovanni stopped to talk to so many people I began to find it an effort to keep smiling. As he was a priest there was hardly a person we passed whom he did not know. Everyone wanted to shake his hand and he theirs, which inevitably led to another long conversation about very little.

To the great relief of my soles we eventually made it to the community centre. There were many young boys horsing around in the playground and inside little girls were crowded round tables colouring in books. Don Giovanni took me upstairs to a small but clean room with two bunk beds. He was a shy man and was gone almost before I had time to say thank you, leaving me to find the bathroom for myself.

Just as I had got into bed there was a clatter of walking poles and Jan and a stranger burst through the door. Don Giovanni hovered in the background looking uneasy. I got up, bracing myself for a limp hug and Jan kissed me several times. The man behind him was Thierry who was so excited at meeting me that his coordination went haywire and he almost whacked the bottom of my chin with his walking pole as he went to shake my hand. They asked if I would mind them and Claude sharing the room and, giving me little time to answer although of course I said yes, they turned to Don Giovanni and said in broken Italian, 'Alice doesn't mind – she's our friend.' And so the room was taken over by three over sixty year olds who washed and changed and chatted as I got back into bed.

Thierry, the newest recruit, a Belgian, was an extraordinary character. He was thin but broad and completely uncoordinated.

He leapt around the room like an oversized monkey and insisted on trying to understand everything I said including things that were merely passing comments and not really meant for conversation. He spoke with such sincerity, saying things which he would have been better off just thinking. Peering at me in the bottom bunk he told me I was beautiful and looked so young. Following it up with 'I am sixty-one years old but I am in good shape, very, very good shape.' When I told him I had met so many generous people along the way he said, 'Of course women want to mother you but men want to take you home for other reasons.' The voicings of his subconscious mind, however inappropriate, did make me laugh.

They all went out to dinner and I tried to get to sleep but even if I had, Jan's mounting of the bunk above me would have shaken me awake. That night Thierry snored almost as loud as he farted. All night long his gastric noises filled the dark room and in the morning when he asked if I slept well I told him it was a difficult thing to do with him in the room. He said, 'Yes, last night I drink lots of red wine and after red wine I sleep well and I snore all night long.'

Berceto - Pontremoli. September

I left Bercetto early and dripped tears through the quiet streets, longing to have arrived in Rome and be done with the journey. My head ached with tiredness so I kept to the road all day for fear of running out of energy on a forest track. I went up and up a road too steep for even a bicyclist to remain on their seat and arrived at the Cissa path as the solo bar was opening. From the top at 1041 metres I crossed over the border into Tuscany and followed a winding road that descended for 805 metres through the forest canopy of the upper valley of the Magra River. With two very sore soles and a pain of a left foot I arrived in Pontremoli at the bottom of the valley and the confluence of the rivers Magra and Verde.

Pontremoli is an old medieval town shadowed by the castle of Piagnaro which sits on a hill at the Northern end of the town. Being the last major town on this side of the Cissa Pass, it has suffered a history of wars and has consequently been rebuilt many times. It is thought the original fortress was built between the 9th and 10th centuries and subsequently restored and reconstructed up until the 14th century. Having read that pilgrims could sleep in one of two converted rooms in the castle, I headed up the narrow alleyway and sat in the baking sunshine waiting for the gates to re-open after lunch. A charmless man finally opened the entrance and I followed him through a large stone tunnel into his office where he got out a key, and then he led me to a narrow room with eight beds high in the castle walls. Most of the fortress is a ruin but it has been sympathetically restored so one can walk up gangways, round the walls and into the turrets, getting a great view across the slate roofs of the town in one direction and up into the blue mountains in the other. Shortly after I had arrived Thierry, Jan and Claude came huffing and puffing into the room next to me.

Desperate to sleep, I was in bed very early. Jan came and sat in my room for a bit complaining about how slow Claude was and asked if I would walk with him tomorrow. I fell asleep before it was even dark outside. I always need to get up in the night to go to the loo and here it meant walking along an open-air stone corridor looking out over bare castle ruins but I had prepared myself for it, knowing I would need to. The first time I went I was not at all frightened and quickly fell back to sleep again. However, in the night, in my very dark narrow stone room I was woken by the whisper of a voice in my ear. Someone, bending down over my bottom bunk with a presence of their head right up close to mine was whispering in English 'You're so brave, so very brave'. Initially I wondered what an earth one of the 60+ year olds was doing in my room so late. It was too dark to see anything but I could sense them close to me. So close I couldn't raise my head. Stuck to my pillow, I shouted 'Get out'. There was no response and absolutely no noise, not even a rustle. The dark room smothered me with its chilling atmosphere and turning towards the wall I lay frozen, my heart beating rapidly. Through sheer lack of movement I fell back to sleep and didn't wake until my alarm went off at 6:30am. I got up to brush my teeth and returning, having woken up with a splash of cold water, I looked out over the fortress wall to a pitch black sky with stars shining bright. Disconcerted I returned to my room and turned on my telephone to check the time. Goodness knows how but my watch had gone an hour forward in the night. I lay in bed waiting for the sun to rise and by the time it finally became light enough to leave I was longing to reach the next bed and make up for such a restless night. Jan came out of his room just as I was making my way down the steps of the ruin. He asked me to wait for him and I said I would meet him on the bench by the cathedral. Twenty minutes passed and the longer I waited the more lethargic I became, which in turn made me cry. Having run out of patience, I set off without him.

Pontremoli - Aulla. September

I so want to go home. This whole experience makes me miss my family and friends more than I knew I could. Life is too precious to spend time in a country where you do not feel completely safe. I have now been walking for 60 days and I long to be back in the nest of home comforts. Before I began this journey I vowed to make no contact with friends, as I was eager to detach myself from the everyday and let my mind run free. However I now craved company and fresh thoughts but I knew that if I started contacting friends I would not experience what it is like to be truly alone and that, in a self-destructive way, intrigued me.

I had to stop after an hour, as my feet were sorer than usual, having been on the tarmac two days in a row. I drank coffee and munched my way through chewy sweets as if they were a bunch of grapes, desperate to get some energy. Jan came bouncing up to me, fed up with Claude who held him up this morning before deciding to take a bus. The extraordinary Thierry then arrived but did not stop for long. The sight of him walking off made me laugh so much. Imagine an office chair on wheels with a wide seat and arm-rests. Put in a large-framed, 61-year-old with saggy nipples and glasses that exaggerate the size of his head, arms on the arm-rests but bent at such an angle that the elbows jut out as if they are disjointed. Dangle walking poles from his weak wrists and tell him to get from A to B with just his feet. This was Thierry and with the energy he must expend it is no surprise his bottom jaw always hangs open.

I spent the rest of the day walking with Jan who was nice but for some reason he does make my skin crawl. If only the spring in his feet rubbed off on his dry character I think I would enjoy his company more, but the immaculately trimmed moustache, stiff on his top lip, and clothes fitting so perfectly that over-indulgence was unthinkable, deprived him of any sex appeal. Not that I tend to find 63-year-olds attractive, but if someone has sex appeal they are always more fun to spend time with.

We met Claude waiting on a bench by the river Marga on the way into Aulla and headed to L'Abbazia di San Caprasio to find a bed. Two friendly monks welcomed us and the elder of the two took us to a large municipal building on the second floor of which was a room with fourteen beds and a bathroom. We each chose a bed in opposite corners of the room. I took off my boots and lay down, falling fast asleep almost immediately.

When I got up to shower Jan and Claude seemed to be asleep. I changed and as I went to leave the room Jan leapt up and followed me out. He wanted to go for a beer. I said I was going to the supermarket and he remarked, 'Don't you want to come with me?' I was exhausted so replied saying all I wanted was to find food and go back to bed. He strode off down the street and I went to have a look at the church.

L'Abbazia di San Caprasio, founded in 884 and originally dedicated to Santa Maria, is the oldest building in Aulla, a town ruined in the World Wars. The most recent—post World War II—renovation of the Abbey restored the original structure with three naves. The interior of the church resembled the aftermath of a recent flood; however, with a light on in the apse I went in to have a look. Beneath the altar, housed behind glass, were the few skeletal remains of San Caprasio and in an ornate box to the side were many more bits of bone including a skull belonging to the 4th century San Severo. I went on through a door into the Abbey where there was a museum dedicated to passing pilgrims.

The remains of San Caprasio, a 4th century hermit from the Lerins Islands in Provence, were believed to have been brought to Aulla in the 10th century; however, over the years they had been lost amongst the rubble and renovations of the ramsacked church. In 2003 during the excavations on the hunt for the tomb of San Caprasio the archeologists unearthed an unexploded bomb from the Second World War. The bomb was removed and revealed underneath was a tomb, the bones of which were carbon-dated to the 4th century and believed to be those of San Caprasio. What a miraculous coincidence.

I went to find the helpful monks from earlier and ask for directions to the supermarket. Inside the cloister I found the younger one. His dog collar was loose around his neck, which was ironically seductive. It didn't help that he was also very attractive in that dark rather more Spanish than Italian way. I followed him to his office as we tried to communicate in French. He drew me a map of how to get to the supermarket and insisted I took his bicycle. It is the first time I have been anywhere near riding a bike in months and faced with the option I said I would rather walk. As I went to leave he stood up and we brushed past each other so close I honestly thought he was going to kiss me and for fear of doing the wrong thing I did not look up.

That night I was asleep before Jan and Claude had left for dinner. I knew that next day I was going to see the sea and I just could not wait. The thought of it made me long to be in it, so I set my alarm early thinking it might just be possible.

Aulla – Marina di Massa. September

Today my sole aim was to try to get my feet in the sea. I left just as it was begining to get light, the clouds were low in the valley and I had to walk two hours up hill before I began to get above them. When I eventually saw the crest of the mountain I could hardly wait to be there, desperate for a view of the coast. On top there was the most magical view out over a sea of soft white clouds with mountain peaks rising above it and a huge bright shining ball of hot sunshine. It was so pure it softened the blow of not seeing the sea. I had to go down back into the clouds before climbing up another peak over the final ridge of the Apennines and into Liguria. As I went up a track through the woods the horseflies relentlessly bit my bottom through my lycra shorts. I slapped at my behind never getting them but amused by the indirect encouragement I was giving myself.

After a long steep climb past the medieval hill top towns of Bibola and Ponzano Superiore I eventually reached a spectacular view of the Ligurian plains surrounding the city of Sarzana and the estuary of the River Magra. The Mediterranean was a thin strip in the distance so far away I almost lost hope of making it today. I stopped and bound up my left foot with sticky tape to try and give it extra support before the steep decent to Sarzana. When I reached the city I had a race against time to try and find the tourist office before it closed for lunch. I went in circles asking so many people for directions and eventually realised it was the wooden hut in the middle of a square, which looked like nothing other than a wooden hut in the middle of a square. The woman inside was hopeless. She said she knew nothing about accommodation on the coast, as it was back in the region of Tuscany and her office only covered Liguria. My guidebook leads one through the hills rather than along the coast so that was also no help. The woman gave me a map, which covered enough of the area around Sarzana to get me to the coast, but I could not tell how big the road was. I tried asking her if it was safe to walk along but her English was not up to it and she just kept pointing at a big blue road sign, which said Marinella di Sarzana.

I left Sarzana, a town full of wonderful architecture, on the main road to the sea. Desperate to reach the salty water, I did not even stop to buy any food. Out of the town the road got dangerously big very rapidly and I knew it was irresponsible to continue but my desire to swim got the better of me. Out of the mountains the flat view was hazy with heat and, it being Saturday, there were a lot of other people in fast cars speeding to the beach. The road was flanked by crash barriers and there wasn't even a verge to stand on. Fortunately there was a bicycle slipstream and I decided to please the Italians and walk with the traffic. The first sign I passed said 7 kilometres to the sea.

I knew I was being reckless but I really did not want to turn around and in 90 minutes, if I survived the traffic, I would be there. As I was mulling over what a crazy decision this was and that I would never ever tell anyone, a black estate car overtaking me put on its indicator and pulled into a rough lay-by that seemed to appear out of nowhere. It was a little further on and as I approached I said to myself if they offer me a lift then *yes* to a family, *no* to a man. Sure enough the window slid down in that smooth manner that tinted windows have. First I looked to the back where there was the friendliest smile and a beautiful brown-eyed woman sitting next to her equally beautiful brown-eyed baby. I turned to the driver who smiled from behind dark glasses in a totally friendly non-pervy way. His English was good but I had been so concerned with their appearance that I had not listened to what he was saying. 'The sea, the sea, the sea!' I exclaimed and he patted the empty front seat. In I got with my rucksack blocking the view and we nattered all the way to the sea where they had a private parking spot and a boat. They were the nicest Italians I have met so far and when it came to saying goodbye we all kissed and hugged, and they didn't even flinch at my hot sweaty appearance.

I walked smiling out to sea, laughing at the hideousness of the coast I was so desperate to get to. It is one long strip so covered in people you can barely see the sand. The beaches all have a charge and the fat people waddle back and forth from scruffy campsites to deck chairs stopping in the endless pizzerias and bars in-between. A huge boulevard runs parallel to the beach. I joined several under-dressed people strutting up the pavement whilst I looked for somewhere half decent to stay. Struck by hunger I stopped in a pizzeria and ate such a big pizza it went straight through me before I had time to leave.

The whole narrow area between sea and mountains is covered in houses and each town merges into another with very little to distinguish them. Eventually, out of Liguria and back into Tuscany, I made it to a slightly smarter-looking town of whitewashed buildings with green painted shutters. There wasn't a campsite in view and the beach now said *Strada Privata*. I left the boulevard up a side street into the centre of Marina de Massa. I walked up the immaculate raised front steps of the first hotel I came to and asked the man how much for one night. '90 euros.' My face fell. I have got so used to paying nothing for a bed that 90 euros seemed far too much. He looked at me with pity and said 70 euros with breakfast. I was so flattered by his attempt to help that I accepted straight away. The room he took me to was a bombsite but I communicated that I would change and go to the beach while it was cleaned.

I confidently walked straight past the *Strada Privata* sign, on to the beach and left my towel and book on a wooden deckchair as I floated in the salty sea, flat on my back, toes peeping out of the water, bobbing on the gentle waves. If I looked straight up I felt completely alone. It was wonderful. I lay on the deckchair, undisturbed by the beach controller, without an ounce of energy left in me. It was too hot to sleep comfortably so I slumped back to my now clean air-conditioned room and slept in what felt like luxury.

Marina di Massa - Camaiore. September

During the night I heard the distant calls of a disco but nothing was going to draw me out of a deep slumber. Breakfast was like walking into an empty tent with the most sumptuous array of food spread on tables filling half the room. When there is so much choice I get a fear of having to make a decision but with a rumbling tummy as my leader I went for it all. With no other early risers in that empty room, I filled up on a croissant, a pastry, a biscuit with chocolate and peanuts, a sausage, slices of parma ham, a soft-boiled egg and toast layered with cherry jam, a cup of coffee, and two fruit juices in one glass. I then left and followed the coast for two hours watching jiggling bottoms overtake me and listening to the whirr of men in lycra, not a woman among them.

I reluctantly left the flat of the coast to head back into the foothills of the nearby Apennines. It was Sunday but much to my relief the tourist office in Pietrasanta, a small medieval town just north of the coast, was open. I mustered all my charm and enthusiasm to get the hairy woman in the tourist information kiosk to persevere with booking me into a B&B in Camaiore, a small town further on. Having succeeded she told me that to get there I needed to follow the red and white signs of the Via Francigena. Confident in the knowledge of a bed ahead I sat on the pavement drinking several cans of coke and absorbing the calm atmosphere of Pietrasanta.

Pietrasanta is a small town with narrow cobbled streets spread out like long straight legs from the Piazza del Duomo with its beautiful Romanesque cathedral of white marble. In the 15th century when Michelangelo Buonarroti realised the beauty of the nearby marble mined from the Carrara quarries, Pietrasanta grew in importance as a town and many foundries were opened. Today the town remains a centre for sculptors and artists alike and the streets are ornamented with modern bronze sculptures set against the architecture of a prosperous past.

I was on my way to Lucca, passing through the last few rolling hills beneath the Appenine Mountains and looking forward to a rest in Camaiore. A lot of the way was on roads which I dislike for many reasons but one is the hassle from male drivers. An old man pulled over in his scruffy yellow box of a car. He lent over and opened the side door as I passed. I stopped to say hello and he tapped the spare seat next to him. I said no and he began talking at me in Italian. I said no again and he raised his voice and hit the empty seat. The more I said *no* the crosser he got. I left him to his temper and walked on, his parting shot having been to stamp on the accelerator and take off with as much speed as his rattlebox allowed. Italian men really are something else. Even if they don't stop, every time they drive past you, you can guarantee seeing their necks craned and their reflection glaring back at you from their wing mirror. I am now so used to it that it makes me smile but to begin with it did frighten me.

The scene outside a launderette soon cheered me up; the car doors were wide open, the music booming out and a large woman dressed in pink was sweeping the leaves outside her shop, dancing with the broom as if it were a microphone. Totally unselfconscious, she was going for it and clearly having great fun. How I would love to be half as liberated.

Today was very hot and I sweated so much I thought perhaps I had a fever. By the time I got to Camaiore I was more desperate for a shower than ice cream so went straight to my B&B. It was a scruffy building behind huge electric gates, one of which creaked open when I buzzed the intercom. I made my way towards a woman hovering on the doorstep. She smiled without warmth and greeted me in a sickly sweet manner and a tone so fake she seemed the type who could slit your throat without flinching. Inside it felt like a time-warp. The house was ancient and immaculate as if the secrets of history were hidden under the floorboards and inescapable. It frightened me into conforming for fear of what might happen otherwise. I was sure that this small family with one son was hiding something but when I quickly realised I had lost my passport I was at their mercy and had little control.

Italy has some rules that, no matter what the circumstances, people abide by. Needing a passport to stay anywhere is one of them. Having shown me a large bedroom the woman asked me to come downstairs with my 'identità'. I emptied my rucksack searching for my passport, which was not in the plastic case with my few important belongings. Realising I must have left it in the hotel in Marina di Massa I got the name off the receipt and went downstairs. I knocked on the kitchen door and pushed it open. There I met the intimidating husband and neurotic son who thankfully spoke good English. I looked towards the son whose pupils dilated as I told him my mistake. He proceeded to translate the issue to his parents who in turn looked at me as if I had committed a serious offence. The boy, who clearly had a disturbed character, must have been about my age. While his mother sat at the table and father impatiently searched online for the telephone number of the hotel, he stood hands trembling, transferring his weight from one flip-flop to the other which created a metronomic sucking sound on the linoleum floor, adding to the intensity of the atmosphere.

Having found and called the hotel, the son translated that my passport was there and a copy of it would be faxed over by five o'clock tonight. I went upstairs and had a shower before knocking on the kitchen door again. The raised voices went quiet and I opened the door to fixed smiles. I said to the boy I would pay what they wanted for someone to drive me to Marina di Massa. The mother, who apparently didn't speak English, looked furiously at the boy and said something. He stared at me and said that was not a possibility. I then said I would get a bus or a train but, being Sunday, no buses ran and there was no train station nearby. He went on 'We have rung the police, you must write a declaration.' I sat down at the head of the table. The mother, sitting on my right, handed me a pen and pushed a blank piece of paper in front of me. The son, with the non-stop sucking noise of his feet, standing to my left, held a jittering piece of paper from which he dictated as I wrote: I myself, Alice Warrender, born in Forres on the 1st of January 1983, currently living at: Minuntion, Pinwherry, Ayrshire.

The mother stretched across and held her pointed finger in the centre of my bit of paper as the son continued and I wrote in capitals: DECLARATION

The copy of the passport that I show you is the exact copy of the original. My passport is at Hotel Tirreno, in Marina di Massa.
before signing and dating it.

I looked up and laughed out loud but they remained deadly serious. The son photocopied the piece of paper, giving me the copy and his mother the original.

The mother then asked me to recite my proposed itinerary for the next week as she wrote it down very neatly on a fresh bit of paper. I was completely baffled at the same time as feeling increasingly uneasy. The son told me I must return to my room and that when the fax of the passport came I would go with his mother to the police station.

I felt far out of my depth in a situation that was running away from me. The unbelievable control of the place almost got a grip of me but inspired by their obstinacy I returned to the kitchen without knocking and stood facing both son and mother and in a raised voice said, 'My mother insists I get my passport today and she will pay whatever it costs. I need a taxi number.' It was as if they thought I might hit them. Within seconds the mother was on the telephone and the son told me a taxi would be here shortly.

There was a noise of a car and we all went out onto the doorstep. There was fat ancient Angela, who had a grim smile full of rotten pointy teeth and a turquoise toweling nighty that matched the colour of her mobility car. Having shaken hands, she opened the door for me in professional taxi style and I slid in to a heavily hoovered, dirt stained seat. Off we set for Marina di Massa. I soon gave up on trying to make conversation as my comments invariably led to questions from her which to her mounting irritation I could not answer. We rattled back over the 25 kilometres, overtaking everything regardless of oncoming traffic or corners. She chewed her gums and spat out of the window whilst picking her nighty out of her folds. After an hour of retracing my steps we got to the hotel. Angela careered on, looking for somewhere to park. I pointed at the curb and managed to get her to wait, door open, leg up, air between her legs, as I ran back to the hotel and retrieved my passport, holding it with a grasp I never wanted to open. 35 euros later and back in Camaiore I wondered what all the fuss was about.

Having not eaten since breakfast I was now calm enough to feel the hunger in my tummy. I sat in a dark church waiting for the restaurants to turn their lights on. At seven o'clock I entered an empty room and ordered unconventionally. When the food arrived I immediately felt far from alone: seafood spaghetti, cannollotti beans, roasted vegetables of many colours, olive oil and fizzy water. The fuller I got the more tired I became.

I slept in the most enormous room in a large brass double bed and by breakfast the woman's sickly sweet manner and way of saying my name, drawing out the *s* as if she had a forked tongue, made me long to be away from this odd place. But first there was a table laid as if breakfast, lunch and dinner were coming all at once. Everything that I ate came with a long explanation interpreted by the son. Following the routine of lunch or dinner I went for savory first, broccoli tart, and then worked in a semi circle until I had had at least a corner of everything, ending with a fig stuffed with nutella. I got up and got out with one final wave as Mother and son stood in the arch of the door with fixed smiles.

Camaiore - Lucca. September

As I was leaving Camaiore early this morning I was walking towards the front of a workman's truck. At the tailgate were two men in luminous overalls engrossed in something one of them was doing. As I walked past one grinned at the other with eyes full of excitement as the other fumbled with his camera in a rush to take my picture. I did not have the courage to smile back. They took the picture and wolf-whistled behind me. Thank goodness the rest of today was mainly cross-country.

Just after I had stopped to go to the loo in the woods I saw a man ahead of me on the path. Edo was on his first of 15 days to Rome. We puffed up a hill together and I left him resting at the top with the name of his hostel in Lucca lodged in my head and keen, however nice he was, not to share a room and give pleasure to yet another old man.

I walked up the right bank of the River Serchio into Lucca, the first place on my journey I had been to before, and what a feeling it was to walk under the arch and into the city. I knew the streets, the bars, and the restaurants. I even took a detour just to pass the hotel where we had stayed the year before. The lanes were crammed with tourists and I pushed my way through them to a hostel on the other side of the city. It was lunchtime and another two hours before the hostel opened so, lying against my rucksack on a scruffy patch of grass with my head to the sky, blind to whatever passers-by thought, I read my book and waited.

I was followed in to the hostel by an older couple but thankfully I got a room with several beds to myself. I wandered nostalgically round the city re-visiting all I had loved before. I visited the Duomo di San Martino, headed up Via Fillungo to La Piazza dell'Anfiteatro and out onto the intact city walls, walking above the city on a turf mound and heading back in to the wonderful church and market in Piazza San Michele. Worn out, I sat in a small square round the corner eating ice cream in the exact spot from which Papa had painted Puccini's house the year before.

I tried to remain out until dinner but was too exhausted and found myself dragging my sore feet back to the enormous bedroom with a bag of focaccia, as if I had not eaten it for lunch. I lay on the big brass bed longing to be in Rome and have this all behind me. There are only 415 kilometres left to go, that is less than a quarter of the whole journey but it carries so much weight. The less the distance gets the more I doubt I am going to make it. There is no way I could do it without believing in God. No matter what He is or if He is at all, by believing in a greater good it stops me being selfish and giving in. I know that if I am doing it for God I will not stop until I get there and I continue to pray for his help through Our Lady. She gives me strength and comfort to carry on without which I would struggle and pity myself. If I were doing it for me I would have missed the point and stopped way back but in continuing I get so much more out of it than I would have ever imagined. It is how to take this philosophy into every day life that challenges me. I feel myself getting excited about Rome and thinking about life after that and I find myself wrapped in my own wants and not looking to God for help. I must do something, a career, which needs some power from the outside and that way I will never forget that we are not in control of our own destiny. I am still searching for the answer to how I am going to go about life after this but I now know I will rise to the challenge of making painting the purpose of my life. Simple commitments like this bring me closer to knowing that the overall structure is there if I just stick at trying to find it.

Lucca – Ponte a Cappiano. September

I woke early with a scratchy throat. Unable to get back to sleep I left Lucca just as it was beginning to get light. A man on the other side of the road shouted out at me and beckoned for me to cross. I went over to him but I had no idea what he was saying. We were standing in front of a kebab shop and he shouted through the door. A man stood in the doorway rambling in Italian and then went back inside. I was confused but the old man was not going to let me go just yet and continued to talk at me as if suddenly I might start speaking back. He called in the house next door and a large man with chest puffed out came to join the conversation. He turned to me and said in English 'You need my help?' I leapt at the opportunity to say something 'I'm walking the Via Francigena from Canterbury to Rome and today I go to Ponte a Cappiano' He said rather more gruffly 'You need my help?' The instigator looked on with a broad grin as if it was all thanks to him that the conversation was in such full flow. I looked at them both with raised eyebrows and smiled as I said thank you. Not that there was anything to thank them for but it gave me an exit and on I went.

As the sun rose the day became boiling hot. I stopped in Altopascio where I drank coke in the shade. My soles hurt even more than usual and I began to think my body really was going to give in; however, I was keen to make it to Ponte a Cappiano where I knew there was an ancient hostel which I wanted to stay in. I pushed on for another hour and knowing the distance left of the day was manageable I stopped in Galleno, out of the heat, in a scruffy roadside café. There were three men propping up the bar that I am sure talked about me from the moment I arrived to the moment I left. As I was paying, too tired to attempt Italian, I thanked the woman in English. One of the men said 'English', 'Yes, I'm Scottish'. He was a black beanpole starring at me through his wire frame glasses, lips parted to give his yellow teeth a good look, and said 'My name is Ass, I shake my ass everyday'. 'How nice' I replied. 'You know ass, yes, ass is English and Scottish'. 'Yes ass is English and Scottish'.

I climbed up over the ridge of Le Cerbai dripping sweat as if I had a fever and descended into the valley of the River Arno. The pilgrim hostel in Ponte a Cappiano is located in a bridge over the River Usciana. The origin of the bridge dates back to Roman times; however, the present bridge was built in the 16th century to replace one destroyed in 1325 during a war between Lucca and Florence. Cosimo de'Medici, an important patron of the arts, oversaw the rebuilding of the bridge, a drawing of which by Leonardo da Vinci is now in the Royal Collection at Windsor.

As I waited for Monika to find the keys of the hostel in her desk drawer I stood engrossed by a huge rat, slowly sniffing its way through a patch of grass outside the window. There is something about the weight in the backend of a rat that makes it particularly revolting. I shuddered and pointed but Monika who was now trying to explain the handful of keys to me did not even move to the window to see what had lit up my face.

After the experience in Pontremoli I promised myself I would not stay in any more castles if the opportunity arose and perhaps I should have thought a little more cautiously about staying in a 16th century hostel as inside it had an uneasy air to it. I was the only person staying which was no surprise but it did make my room of ten beds and dining room—with seating for over 20—a very empty space for one person to rattle around in. I washed in the most hopeless shower where I had to point the head towards the doorless door to get the few drips to drop down on me. I then went to the only shop in town to mosey over the counter and pick out some food for dinner. I could hardly bring myself to sit at one of the empty tables in the dining room, as there was a pungent smell of something bad in the air. Searching round for olive oil which, above loo paper or washing up liquid, you can always guarantee finding in an Italian hostel, I found the door of the fridge ajar and retched at the scene inside. There were several half-eaten packets of old food now alive with mould. I shut the door, flung the windows open and ate the delicious things I had bought doused in extra virgin olive oil.

The night was terrible. A combination of an angry wind, a slightly frightening atmosphere and persistent mosquitoes meant I had very little sleep. I was up late in the night, wandering the stone corridors, shutting all the windows and shutters that I had opened to air the building. I was frightened but the noise of them banging in the wind was too loud to ignore. Despite creating an intoxicating cloud of mosquito repellant in the bottom bunk, they continued to bite. I would hear their $z \, z \, z$ so close to me but snatching in the dark I never got them. Unable to sleep I lay in bed with my torch in my mouth waiting for them to come into the circle of light. They never came and eventually, worn out by the effort of holding a torch between my lips, I nodded off.

Ponte a Cappiano – San Miniato. September

Lifting my head off the pillow this morning was the hardest it has been in months. My throat was very sore and I felt like one big heavy reluctant lump being pulled up onto two very delicate swollen pads of feet. I walked five kilometres and stopped in a dreary café in Fucecchio. Unable to muster the energy to carry my coffee to the colourful chairs on the pavement, I sat on one of two chairs in the narrow space between the bar and the wall. It felt as though my head were at sea and my eyes stared blindly into the middle distance. I ate a cream dough-nut, which was delicious and soft on my throat, drank coffee purely for the caffeine and poured a whole bottle of fizzy water into myself.

On my way out of the town I went into a fruit shop full of fruit and of course flies. A man in front of me, I think, asked how far I had come. I opened my book and pointed at the number 1704 kilometres. He looked up to me as if to say Stupid girl you don't understand do you? I smiled at him, thinking I do not blame you for not believing me, and he left the shop. I had chosen a cloudy red, giant, strawberry-shaped apple from the top shelf. 40 cents and the man went to put it in a bag. 'Non,' I said, motioning to convey I would eat it straight away. The inquisitive woman watching from a loose curtain behind the counter said she would wash it. I stepped out and bit into the crunchiest, sweetest, juiciest apple I could have imagined and ate it before the water on the skin had time to dry.

Battling against the realisation that I had a fever and knowing I had to stop, I struggled on nine further kilometres to San Miniato, a small historic town situated on a hill above the river Arno and characterised by a tall tower, which is all that survives of the 13th century castle. How I got lost going to the top of a hill I do not know but thankfully when I got to the Convento di San Francesco, despite a convention, they had a spare room for me. It is charming; two beds, a bathroom and a view down on to the cloister. With a very sore throat and a heavy head I got straight into bed and fell fast asleep between sneezes, a very odd thing to be doing in such heat.

I woke disorientated and my head on the pillow feels more like the lead doorstop. I am staring at the white-washed walls going from shivering goose pimples to claustrophobic stuffiness, just waiting. Waiting to feel better and willing the hours to go slowly so that I, have time to catch up. At three-thirty I dizzily found my way to the chemist and sat on a chair inside the door while the queue subsided. It was my turn. I tried my best through a smile to communicate the pain of my throat, the blocked sinuses, the heavy head and fever. The woman looked at me blankly and I had no idea if she had understood any of it. I hardly had anything left in me to keep trying to win over her nice side. I wanted to cry, drop down on the floor and say I have walked from Canterbury, I must get to Rome and I will take whatever you recommend to get me better enough to continue. I know it is my fault, I know I am mad, I know I am ill but I need to reach St Peter's Square as there is something in the air for me there and I can only get it by walking the last little bit. It is at times like this that you want someone to know you so well they will catch you as you fall.

I left with a small bottle of turquoise pills and a throat spray. The journey was hard enough anyway and being ill really frustrated me. My only other hope was to go to Mass. It was in a small side chapel off the Church of San Francesco in whose monastery I was staying. I felt so ill I had to sit throughout.

Longing to be back in bed I went inside for dinner which was part of the deal. The dining room was huge and decorated with 17th century frescoes, a large one on the back wall showing the Last Supper. I was first in, shortly followed by lively Edo. He shook me by the hand and patted me on the shoulder as if to say we are two of the same kind. I sat opposite him on a table with four monks. The one next to me was the man who had said Mass. He was bad-tempered and we didn't communicate once, both filling our water glasses alternately. Opposite him was a very large simple-looking man with a smile that longed for one in return and next to him was a wonderful-looking man in a long black habit tied with white rope. He was round but solid and his fat nose splodged onto his face was its main feature. His bald head was so thick that the arms of his spectacles curved above his ears only just reaching to hook round the very top of them. It really was as if Chaucer had written him into the evening. Opposite him and two to my left was a well-fed young-looking man who every so often would glance up the table at me and interpret what I was trying to say but not once did he join in the conversation. Behind us was a table of twenty-four medieval history graduates here on convention with their professor, a tall, thin, bolt upright man with two bulbous warts on his right cheek and one equally risen from the surface on the right side of his neck. Before we sat down to eat Edo introduced himself to the professor and then pointing at me told him I had walked all the way from Canterbury. His long legs carried him rather too close to me where he hovered while grace was said. While I longed to sit down he held my shoulder and asked if I was following Sigeric's route. 'Yes,' I replied with not an ounce of enthusiasm left in me. His face froze and staring down at me he said in a heavy German accent 'I must present you to my students'. I cowered and said in a hesitant tone, 'No, no; maybe wait until after dinner.' His hand was already in the air silencing the room and calling everyone to attention. He spoke in Italian for what seemed like several minutes as I stood going bright red, his hand still on my shoulder and my full concentration on trying not to faint. Finally there was a lot of clapping and very embarrassed by the undue attention I said thank you to the room and sunk into my chair round a table with Edo and the monks.

At dinner I barely spoke. Edo had fun guessing my age, settling for 18. When I said I was 28 he got carried away in telling me how beautiful I was. Thank goodness none of the monks spoke English. The simple monk smiled at me throughout dinner to the point that his fork mostly missed his mouth. The monk with the thickset bald head kept signalling Edo to fill up my wine glass and the more his eyes glazed over the more frequent his attempts to get me to drink became. Dinner was over in quick refectory style and as soon as the first monk left the room the professor was at my side.

He wanted to see the maps I used. I told him I only had a book and the maps were very bad but this did not stop him asking so I went upstairs and brought him my book. He looked at it intensely and said 'Don't you get lost?' I told him I get very lost but that when I am lost I meet the nicest people. Slowly interpreting in his head what I said he then smiled. He continuously referred to my pilgrimage as marching and said in a heavy German accent made it sound very military. 'You like to march; you march the ancient route of Sigeric; you march every day; you march alone?' He went on and on about bloody marching and then was silent, just staring at me with eyes that looked as if he was calculating something in his head. I balanced myself with one hand on the back of the chair as I looked up at him with drowsy eyes and a head aching for bed. He eventually said in his thick German accent, 'I am thinking. I know a man who wrote an article on the ancient marching routes in Italy and I am trying to work out how to put you in touch. Where will you be in ten minutes?' Fast asleep in bed I wanted to say but instead I told him I would be 'here', exactly where I was in the now empty dining room. He strode out of the room.

I went to find the monks who were slumped around a table in the hall watching *You've been Framed* with Edo. The simple one smiled at me and stood up. I told Edo I felt very ill and please would he tell the monk. The monk then disappeared and returned with a telephone. I was to plug it in by my bed and if I needed anything in the night I could dial 3 and he would come. This made me feel so much better immediately and I said goodnight. The monk shook my hand, the other three mumbled with their eyes still glued to the TV and Edo leapt up, shook my hand and pulled me towards him cupping my head and giving me a kiss on both cheeks. Reluctant to wait for the German, I headed upstairs.

My room was immediately at the top of the stairs but as I got to the door I heard a brisk walk coming down the nearby corridor. I peaked round the corner and there in the dark was the professor. I pushed the timed light switch, as he came round the corner apologising that his friend was not answering the telephone and that sadly he could not put us in touch. Hugely relieved I thanked him for trying. He then went into a slow monologue about his passion for medieval marching routes. I stood leaning against the cold stone wall and as he went on I ever so slowly let my head tilt backwards until I could have almost shut my eyes and fallen asleep. While I was longing for my room directly behind him, he spoke on into the dark as the lights timed out and we were left in the dim orange glow of the fire exit. He gave me the full history of Sigeric's journey to Rome and back, not missing a single date. He then explained that he was a medieval history professor but had specialised in the ancient European marching routes. He expressed his disbelief at meeting me on his last night and he was just so excited to meet for the first time someone marching the whole of Sigeric's route. I lost concentration and began thinking if he doesn't stop perhaps I can slip into my nighty and he can sit on the end of my bed, just there behind him, and then he can talk as much as he likes and I can fall fast asleep. Finally he stuck out his hand and grasped mine, taking a long time to let go. Within seconds I was in bed, laying my heavy head on the pillow and just hoping I would wake feeling stronger.

San Miniato – San Gimignano. September

After San Miniato the Italian countryside seemed to open up. I could see for absolutely miles as I tumbled up and down the open plains of rolling Tuscan hills. The ground was bone dry and the mud cracked with thirst as the tracks breathed out dust. I sauntered along ridges, going up and down from one to the other, suffering under the lack of shade. There were far fewer houses than in the overcrowded valleys of Northern Italy and, as I soon realised, a large distance between places to stay and cafés .

It was way too hot to stop without shade, something cypress trees don't offer, and it was four hours before I passed the first café. It did however mean I shrugged off the lethargy of my cold by the time I stopped. Having filled up on coffee, coke and ice cream all at once I suddenly felt a rush of energy and determination to get to San

Gimignano today. The fact that whenever someone mentioned San Gimignano they could hardly get their words out for big gasps of excitement made me keen to combine a desperately needed day of rest with a town about which everyone was so ecstatic.

As I passed through Gambassi Terme, the last place to find a bed before San Gimignano, I decided perhaps it would be sensible to book a bed ahead before I continued. I bounced into a bakery with a big smile saying 'buongiorno' and opening my book on the counter I pointed at a telephone number and held my hand to my ear in the sign of a telephone. I then mimed sleeping on my hand and said 'Oggi e domani', today and tomorrow. The woman behind the counter was very amused and seemed to fully understand what I was asking. Rushing behind the plastic curtain she returned with the telephone and handed it to me. 'No parlo Italiano' I said and handed it back to her at the same time as pointing to the number in my book. Having dialled the number she said a few things in a very long sentence and waited for the reply. Hanging up she looked at me waiting eagerly and said 'pronto'. I bought a slice of pizza wrapped in paper, thanked her very much and left.

It was a long day and the problem with open countryside was that you could see the town you needed to get to miles in the distance but it never seemed to get any closer. With the fourteen towers of San Gimignano ever so slowly getting nearer I eventually found myself gently stepping in great pain up the steps of the formidable Convento di San Agostino. I rang the buzzer three times before the door opened to a cloister, though the person who let me in remained invisible. I walked through groups of Americans and found a priest behind the till in the gift shop. 'Buongiorno' I said followed by 'Do you speak English?' 'A little,' he replied. I explained that I had telephoned to say I was coming and that I was staying for two nights. He told me I had not done anything of the sort. Slightly taken aback and confused I said 'I telephoned three hours ago'. He told me they didn't take reservations for pilgrims. So, put firmly in my place, I asked whether it would be possible to stay the night. Without a direct answer he asked for my credentials. Looking at my pilgrim passport and reading my address he said out loud to himself 'Ayrshire'. 'Do you know Ayrshire?' I asked with surprise. 'I was born in Elgin.' Amazed, I told him I was born just up the road from Elgin in Forres. He made no comment and in the silence I suddenly exclaimed 'You speak a little English?' 'Just a little,' he said in a now distinguishable broad Scottish accent. What an almighty chip he had on his black shoulder.

I followed him through the cloister, up a staircase, along a vaulted corridor and in through a miniature arched wooden door to a dimly lit room with three short beds all pushed together so they could fit. 'There you go,' he said, turning to leave. 'I am hoping to stay for two nights?' I said questioningly. 'Pilgrims can only stay one night.' I almost broke down and with glassy eyes I said 'I have walked 38 kilometres just to have a day off. Please. I really need to sleep'. He didn't answer me and flapped his way in his black habit back down the long corridor. I took this for a yes.

I slept all the way through until lunch the next day and if I hadn't been hungry or felt that I should see San Gimignano, I could easily have lain in bed all day in the stuffy heat looking at the stained, crumbling white walls. I dragged my heavy head downstairs and past the frescoed walls of the church, out by the steps and fell upon the first restaurant I came to where I ate the most delicious pizza covered in truffle paste with a base so thin and crispy it fell apart on the way to my mouth. No wonder Italians all have pizza ovens built into the outside walls of their houses if they can make them as good as this.

I then wandered into town feeling as drowsy as an African narcoleptic with a lead weight balanced on their head. The streets were as clean as the drum of a washing machine and stuffed full of Americans eating melting ice creams. It feels a lonely place lacking charm. Shopkeepers sit on stools reading magazines or eating until someone happens to go into their shop then they hide whatever it is that has been interesting them and either stare at the floor in a depressed state or watch you as if urging you to buy more beads, linen and pottery. The tourists take endless photographs of the wonderful buildings and quaint streets, filling them with their foreign pleasure and not listening to the heart of the place whose beat is far away, neglected. The town has no sense of community, all gone to money and left without soul. I set out with a smile on my face but it is a difficult thing to keep in a town like this.

Unlike Lucca where life moves in a circle round the nucleus of the city, San Gimignano is all about the tourists. There is no everyday life, no local people, and brown signs on every corner point you toward the various tourist attractions with nothing left to discover. Even the picturesque viewpoints have an arrow leading you to them and various dressed-up men strumming Italian love songs as you gaze out from the city walls. Busloads of people fill the streets, all with cards on strings round their neck identifying which of the many groups they are in. The shop signs are in English *Handmade Ice Cream, Free Wine, Local Cheese* and the tourist office gives out no leaflets on the history of the town and its architecture; instead you can pay for a group tour.

I related most closely to a hot, fed-up-looking West Highland Terrier. It made me laugh when he got feisty with his doorstop equivalent until his owner tugged at the lead with such force he had little option but to give in. I soon passed him again panting, tongue out, up one of the many steep paved streets. No one was paying him any attention and he looked fed up and a long way from home.

In one of the few churches you did not have to pay to go into there was a notice on the door saying *SILENCE, for prayer only. Close the door behind you.* Once inside, the only way to close the door was to slam it. It amused me so much that I hung about watching the shoulders of the prayerful flinching as the people entered. Giving up on San Gimignano I headed back to my room, planning to get up very early and take pictures when the streets were empty.

San Gimignano - Monteriggioni. September

It was another baking hot day rolling over open countryside. The sunflowers whose bright yellow heads had faced the ground in wet France were now light brown from head to toe and stood bent over and shrivelled as if they had aged eighty years in two months. Their sad heavy heads weighing down on thin bodies made me wonder what it is they are still standing for. I walked for 27 kilometres without stopping. The barren lonely countryside stretched for mile upon mile into the distance out of sight. My eyes could not settle on the vacant view, the endlessness of which filled me with insecurity. It was as if I was falling off a high cliff, the bottom too far away to see and the space in-between empty of company. I have lived through all my thoughts, tired of all my jokes, and I am left in the depth of loneliness. I can find nothing in me to lift the weight of depression, which lingers over me like the devil intercepting my journey. There is almost nothing I get up for other than to arrive at the next place. Something has eaten the carrot and the day of arriving in Rome is so far from my imagination that I cannot feel the slightest ripple of excitement inside me any more. I walk just longing to get to the end of another day, reluctant to stop and rest for fear of it dragging on longer than it needs to.

It seems that shooting goes on every day of the week in Italy, over anybody's land and with no precautions. I fear for my life as rabbits and hares are shot in front of me. Camouflaged men linger down dirt tracks and spring up behind trees in woods on my path. Their glaring eyes and feral look frightens me more than the shotgun in their hand or savage dog by their side. The preciousness of life is so vivid and I long to be back close to my family and living less vulnerably.

My legs were getting tired and in the distance, standing on a mound, I could see a miniature town with what looked like a perfect wall surrounding it. I prayed for there to be somewhere to stay, as it looked a fantastic place. Slowly but surely I got closer and closer, climbing up and through the Porta Fiorentine arch of the ancient wall into medieval Monteriggioni. The wall built between 1213 and 1219 and totalling a length of approximately 570 metres follows the natural contour of the hilltop surrounding the small town. Fourteen equidistant towers break it up and there are only two entrance arches, one facing north to Florence and the other south to Siena. These two gates are connected by the main street, which opens up in Piazza Roma, where there is a small Romanesque church and a few restaurants amongst stone houses. Behind the church there was a door that had a notice for pilgrims saying it was open from 2–6 pm. The pleasure in finding out that I could spend the night here had cheered me up. It was only twelve o'clock so I went into a restaurant, which advertised *specialità locali* on a board outside.

I build up my confidence so much to enter restaurants, hot, sweaty and laden with luggage, that it is always too late by the time I have noticed that perhaps it is not the place for me. This time I have ended up in a tented garden, beneath whirring fans, at one of many tables with stiff white tablecloths, in a place full of people, holding an extortionate menu. As I entered, the waitress, dressed for silver service, hardly looked at me, let alone stepped aside to let me through together with my rucksack and stick. I asked a male waiter for a table for one and he pointed at the furthest away single table on the other side of the tented dining room. With my rucksack on my back I pushed between tables of diners and it was only when I took it off that I was able to see how unbelievably filthy it was. It was covered in a thick light brown coating of dust from the dry dirt tracks. It would not fit between the last of the tables so I left it propped up on the floor.

I am desperate for a large glass of red wine to knock the edge off reality. Very quickly the restaurant filled up even more, making me wonder how on earth I was going to get my bag out. As I faced the room I felt so out of place it made me smile. The children are intrigued as they study me with puzzled faces and the parents look with disapproval at my being in their dining room. It is the people who stare at you with blank expressions that really get me. So I sat smiling back at them until they stopped looking. Every time someone tried again out of the side of their eye they would catch my smile and quickly glance down at their plate.

Having chosen without looking at the price, I slowly ate a bowl of spaghetti and a slice of apple tart with smooth vanilla ice cream, passing the two hours I had to wait. When I returned to the pilgrim entrance it was still shut so I went to the tourist office. As I was

asking the woman what I should do, the man behind me in the queue
said 'Could I have seen you in San Miniato and San Gimignano over
the last two days?'. 'Yes,' I replied 'and you will probably see me in
Siena tomorrow'. He looked confused and I told him I was on my way
to Rome. He said they were on a similar bus trip and asked which
group I was with. I said I was alone and that I was walking. He was
so amazed I kept the fact I had come from Canterbury as a secret for
myself. The woman meanwhile made a telephone call and told me to
go back to the door behind the church. There I met William and his
wife who were volunteers running the hostel. They were a French
couple in their seventies and spoke only a little more Italian than me.
I was shown a room with a big double bed to use if I had a sleeping
bag and a slightly more expensive single bed by the side with sheets
if I needed it. I slept for two hours and then dragged myself up to sit
in the main square and write some postcards. As I was struggling to
keep the cards on the table in the wind I saw William crossing the
square. He had come to tell me that another pilgrim had arrived and
he needed my room key. Knowing that the contents of my bag were
strewn across the single bed, I followed him back to quickly tidy the
room. I got everything in order just before a hot sweaty Italian man
with so much hair there was no gap between beard and chest pushed
the door open. We shook hands as I tried to conceal my shock at the
stranger I was going to sleep next to.

I went and sat outside with William and his wife as they waited
for (no more) pilgrims and I came to terms with the image of my new
room-mate. We said very little to one another as I did not understand
them, nor they me. I had run out of energy for elaborate descriptions
so we just sat and watched the time pass. At seven we went into the
kitchen of the hostel and together with the Italian pilgrim we ate
dinner. William's wife had not been slaving away all day although
it was very nice of them to feed us. We had bean and grain mush
piled into a bowl followed by cold pasta tubes with bolognaise sauce
and then grapes so small there was more pip than grape. The Italian
was a peculiar man full of nervous energy. It was as if he was wired
into something, although his long hair was not standing on end. He

would pour and drink water as though in the grip of some strange obsession that if his cup were empty it had to be full, and vice-versa. He spoke enough English to have a bit of a conversation when he wasn't jumping around on his seat. He was travelling to Rome, on a bicycle with the smallest wheels I had ever seen, pulling a homemade trailer. He said it was an experiment although I am not entirely sure what the experiment was.

At eight o'clock I said goodnight and went to bed. It wasn't until eleven when the Italian came in. He slipped in through the door and slept fully clothed making grunting noises in the night and filling the room with his stale smell. At seven o'clock the next morning I crept out leaving him trying to wake up.

Monteriggioni - Siena. September

I felt so utterly exhausted and worn out walking to Siena that I didn't dare stop for fear of not being able to carry on. Four hours later and immediately as I passed through the ancient city walls under Porto Camillia I bought an apricot jam biscuit and an apple slice from a patisserie and sat on a step just back from the pavement wanting to close my eyes and fall asleep then and there. The traffic passed at head height and I looked upon it like a tramp before dragging myself on and pushing through the busy Sunday streets.

I used to reach the end of a day's walking feeling full of achievement and an excitement about carrying on the next morning. But now, subject to my painful feet and exhausted body, I no longer pre-plan where I aim to stop which is no longer a goal but the place where I admit defeat. And I arrive there dreading the days ahead. From the very beginning I have kept no tally of the days and make sure never to write the day of the week in my notebook. To begin with the days and distances went by so quickly but now the final 284 kilometres seems like a mountain that I will never conquer. The countryside changes, the weather changes, the people change, but the monotony of walking has got almost so unbearable that the small distance remaining seems just too much.

Having never been to Siena I headed straight for Il Campo, which was a pretty magnificent sight to walk into and had the longest queue for the tourist information. Before the woman would tell me where there was a convent I had to buy a paper map for 50 cents. This made her slightly more forthcoming and she put a circle round the symbol of a church and moved onto the next person. I pushed myself out through people more worried about losing their place in the queue than getting my rucksack in their face and stood in the sloping shell-shaped square trying to get my bearings.

Heading south from the city centre with a broad view of Tuscan scenery out over the medieval walls, I found the open door of the Convento Santa Luisa pretty easily and sat in a plastic chair in the hall as a nun manned the door. She was taking down numbers of ID cards as many poor people flocking in to eat flashed them at her. Not one person paid their surroundings any attention, neither thanking the nun nor smiling back at me. They were there for one reason and that was to eat.

Another nun, Sister Giorgetta, came and rushed me upstairs past the shower and into a dorm with three bunks. Looking at her watch, she moved her finger round it telling me lunch was at one-fifteen. I showered and lay in bed waiting for half an hour to pass before finding my way to the canteen and sitting round a table with several people: two vain, muscular men, criminals trying to be helped to find a better path; a tarted-up damaged-looking woman, the wife of one of the criminals who had come to visit from Sicily; two boys, volunteers who help with meals for the poor, one of whom was the only person who spoke any English at all; the cook and Sister Giorgetta herself who had shown me to my room. Lunch was help-yourself from large plastic containers of left-overs heated up individually in a microwave controlled by Sister Giorgetta. I remained very silent, drowned in tiredness. Pudding was an overflowing box of offcuts from the local patisserie, and if they had not have looked as though they had been piled up for the rubbish they might have been more appetising. There was a commotion as more pilgrims arrived. I was called to go upstairs. There was Jan, hot sweaty and kissing me four times. 'You must be Alice?' said a Dutch man by his side. I shook his hand and was then also introduced to two young German boys and a perfectly proportioned short Italian man. Thankfully, together with Claude they filled all the bunks so I was shown to a pull-out bed in a small reading room next door. As soon as I had moved my stuff I lay down on the bed and fell fast asleep for several hours.

I woke with a knock at my door telling me it was dinner-time. It was eight-thirty and I knew then I had no energy for tomorrow so went to find Sister Giorgetta who, just by looking at me, could tell I wanted to stay another night. Dinner was another help-yourself to left-overs in plastic containers. This time we were left to it, I and the six other men. They had all teamed up into a group and apart from the young German boys who were heading home tomorrow the rest of them were confident about arriving in Rome in ten days time. I was stumped by their camaraderie. They all had one person who could speak their native language fluently and like teenagers in an all-boys school no one went outside their comfort zone to talk to the girl. I was so self-absorbed in my own loneliness, deepened by fatigue, that I sat jealous of them all drinking wine and alarmed that what I was doing was so uncharacteristic for a young female.

Having brushed my teeth I went to say goodbye to Jan and Claude as their schedule for arriving in Rome was beyond my capability and I was sure not to see them again. I stood at the door of their room saying good-bye, good luck and it was nice to meet you. Jan got up and kissed me while Claude, engrossed in his telephone, gave a nod of his head. That night there was an almighty thunderstorm, as loud as the early morning traffic.

I woke unable to sleep in but feeling so unconfident and vulnerable that I did not want to get out of bed. The familiar symptoms of heavy depression worried me and I knew I had to force myself out of the room. Downstairs I found one place laid for breakfast and in came Sister Giorgetta who gave me a great big hug which subdued the loneliness inside me and filled the space with warmth and security. After a strong cup of coffee and a pastry I headed out into the quiet streets of Siena.

It is early, the shops are shut, and there are few people in the streets, most in suits and the rest a small collection of fresh-faced tourists. Il Campo is clear, I could tear round the whole thing like a free horse, unnoticed; the gelaterie window has a display of hollow boxes empty of colour and the tabac has a grill so indestructible that it makes cigarettes and postcards seem valuable. The white marble steps down to the curving streets need to be descended one at a time, carefully, in order to avoid a rapid slip on the rain-covered marble and a cracked head, death on the steps of the Cathedral. I sit in a bar as it fills up and empties, fills up and empties. I drink black coffee, some with sugar some without, waiting for Mass at ten. When I feel lonely, vulnerable and doubtful, I find company in church. It will give me help and strength to carry on.

I bought a ticket to go inside the enormous black and white marble Duomo di Siena. Begun in the 13th century, the Cathedral has a few Romanesque features but is essentialy an Italian Gothic masterpiece. It was built over the course of the 13th and 14th centuries, with much of the sumptuous interior decoration commissioned in the 15th and 16th centuries when Siena had recovered from the economic crisis of the Black Death, which wiped out two thirds of the city's population. The ornate facade is a worthy entrance for a building which boasts a treasure chest of works by renowned artists. The beauty and artistic decoration is overwhelming and it is a place to spend days not hours. Pisano, Donatello, Michelangelo and Bernini, among others, all left their mark here. Something I particularly liked as I slid my way along the carpet of marble mosaic were the bronze angels of the high altar by Francesco di Giorgio Martini and Giovanni di Stefano. The lightness and grace of their wings together with their reverent postures exuded a tranquilility in which I stood and bathed.

I wandered the streets of Siena with no purpose, eating ice cream for something to do. I went out to lunch, forcing myself to remain in the company of others for fear of my thoughts alone, and for the rest of the day I slept knowing it was just a matter of time before I would be on my way again. I ate dinner alone with sleepy eyes wanting to be back in bed shut out from the world.

Siena - Buonconvento. September

Sister Guietta woke me up knocking on my door at 6:00am to tell me Mass was in the chapel at 6:45. I entered while the rosary was going on and hovered at the back, undecided whether to walk up the aisle and find space in a pew or remain hovering and hope no one turned round. No one turned round and in the break before Mass I found space in a pew. The two nuns in front of me were so old they both curved towards each other and I could feel the strain in their necks as they tried to look up at the priest. I felt so ill and so faint I had to remain sitting for most of the service. I had a thin layer of sweat all over and could feel it building up on my top lip and trickling down my cleavage. When I did stand my trousers were stuck to the backs of my legs and I longed to rush outside and stand in the howling wind as it tunnelled through the street under a heavy unsettled sky. The weather was so terrible it was as if there was tyranny in the air.

After breakfast not one bit of me felt brave enough to leave but I went to find Sister Giorgetta and say goodbye. I pushed twenty euros into her hand and went to kiss her. I could not hold back the tears as she waved from the doorstep and I walked on daunted by the path ahead. Out by the Porta Romana and into the open countryside of the Arbia valley I went.

It was a long way to the first town where I knew there was a hostel. I munched my way through a packet of biscuits as I dragged my feet 30 kilometres along dusty ridges to Ponte d'Arbia. It was a dirty place where the main road went straight through the middle of the town. I could not find the hostel but knowing I was close I went up to an old man sitting in a plastic chair under an arch and pointed at the name in my book as I tried to pronounce it. I had no idea if he could hear me let alone see enough to read it. Suddenly he grabbed me very tightly in a grip around the top of my arm and stood up. His hand was painfully tight so far up my arm I had to stand very close to him. He began to pull me with him up the street as his clasped hand nestled into my bosom. He was much stronger than he looked which frightened me. I gave a great effort to get loose which infuriated him and he tightened his grip even more as my fingers tingled with lack of blood. He forced me off the pavement and round the back of a building and as he pulled my face right into his I ran out of patience. Raising my stick in my other hand at the same time as shaking the arm he was holding with all my might I got free. The old man started shouting out loud as I rushed round the corner back onto the pavement. Out of a dilapidated building came an inquisitive workman. I was so pleased to see another person that I rushed towards him. I opened my book and underlined with my finger the address of the hostel. He pointed at the building behind him, which did not even have a front door on it. I went inside and sure enough upstairs was a room with several mattresses but no doors and no locks. No matter how sore my feet were I was getting out of here.

On I went thirty-five kilometres from Siena to Buonconvento. It was a charming place with little narrow streets, flags hanging from windows and safety in numbers with plenty of people about. The good thing about a frightening experience is the sense of euphoria you get when it is over, and although there were no hotels visible here I was confident about finding a bed. I went to the church which had no obvious Parrocchia but round the back I found an old couple sitting on a bench and after much confusion they pointed up a dead-end street saying 'Parrocchia'. The street had an awning all the way up it so apart from the door at the end I could see nothing above head height. There was an intercom but the name on the buzzer had slipped from view. I pressed it and heard an irate woman shouting from above. I had no idea what an earth to say and there was no possible way she could see me. On the second shout I pushed open a wooden gate in the wall to my left and peered through. There was a very old woman leaning out of a window high up in the building. I stood hoping she would guess what I wanted from my appearance. She pointed at a metal fire escape and disappeared from the window. I climbed the steps and was let in through French windows. Pointing to the left she barked something at me and went back through the door on the right. In I went to a dingy room with three beds and a bathroom. It was dirty but perfect.

With feet almost too sore to walk on even without a rucksack I went to the supermarket, leaving the French doors unlocked. When I returned, laden with food, I felt rather guilty about eating in my bedroom; the French doors would not open. I knocked and knocked but no one came so I went back to the main door and buzzed the buzzer to a predictable shout from the top window. The nun could not understand my key action and instead stared down at me and gabbled away in Italian. I sighed, wondering why on earth she had to get so cross. Finally she said 'Timbro?' and had obviously decided I was asking to get my pilgrim passport stamped. 'Sì,' I smiled back up to her and climbed the metal stairs. Once again she scurried downstairs and opened the French windows. With few words she came into my room, stamped my passport and disappeared again.

Tomorrow was to be a special day. The walk would take me very close to the house of friends of Muma and Papa and they were going to have me to stay for two nights. I had only met one British person in over two months and I longed to have a conversation when I did not need to act, though most of all I looked forward to being wrapped up in a dressing gown, a scented bath, and listening to the contents of my bag going round and round in the washing machine.

Buonconvento - Bagno Vignoni. September

My state of mind was such that even though I had the most spoiling couple of days ahead I could not make myself feel happy. I walked all the way to Torrenieri, up and down dusty tracks, carrying heavy depression. Not one bit of me was light or enjoying it. I felt tired, tired of the enormous effort to find pleasure in being in Italy and tired of the relentless walking with my belongings on my back along lonely dusty tracks with no other footprints. My mind was stale and full of the pain of my left foot and the countdown of kilometres over time. If I was to continue to Rome in this state I would go mad before I got there. I could not go on like this. I continued, one foot in front of the other, but I felt totally empty and alone. Psychologically the prospect of the final days was infinitely daunting, and this lack of belief weighed me down with a solid force.

I stopped in a café with a counter of patisseries and ordered a marmalade-layered pastry, a croissant and some coffee. The cakes arrived with two cups of coffee delivered by a waitress who obviously thought there would be another person coming to share the feast. I ate for two as an old man stared at my body and not my face. I went back out onto the street and sat on the steps of the church to change my socks. I change my socks whenever I stop and it is almost the nicest part of the day. My feet get a taste of freedom and the fresh socks keep them cool a little longer. I walked on effortlessly with a lightness I had not felt in days. I was so happy and the feeling of enjoyment stayed with me all the way to the ancient village of Bagno Vignoni where I arrived with such excitement about seeing Barbara. I sat under the loggia and set up my camera to take a timed photograph of myself. An American voice said 'Gee, we can do that for you.' I got talking to the two women about their 'trip'. Their husbands arrived in matching green shorts. One of the wives exclaimed 'She's walking to Rome from, where did you say you came from?' 'Canterbury.' 'Yeah. Canterbury.' The husbands were both looking into the middle ground outside of our little group, seemingly disengaged and disinterested. Then, turning his head, not looking anywhere specific, one of them said 'That must be fun going for a walk every day.' The wives smiled at me in agreement. 'Yes, well, no, yes, it's hard work but I suppose you could say fun.' They went off to drink wine and I sat leaning against a stone pillar of the loggia overlooking the main square. Unlike most villages the main square here called the Square of Sources is flooded with water contained within a 16th century pool. Since the Middle Ages Bagno Vignoni has been a popular thermal spa whose source comes from the under-ground volcanic rock. The buildings and pools have remained almost entirely intact making it an historically beautiful place.

I saw a hand waving and I jumped up and waved too, walking towards it with a ball of excitement inside me. It wasn't Barbara. It was the Americans coming out of a bar led by the waving woman. I looked behind me but no one was there so I carried on towards them. They were off to another town so we said goodbye and I returned to sit up against the stone pillar. A man sat swinging his legs next to me and said 'So, I heard you telling those Americans you're walking. Where are you walking?' 'I'm going to Rome and I started in Canterbury.' He looked unsure but not confident enough to ask where Canterbury was. His wife appeared and we all shook hands and talked about Italy. They were dismayed and disappointed by how dry it was and said if they had known they would not have come all the way from Australia. Suddenly I heard my name spoken questioningly and turned around. There was Barbara right next to me standing on my blind right hand side having been listening to our conversation to gauge whether it really was me or not.

I leapt up and she flung her arms around me. It was wonderful: someone I knew, someone I understood, someone who really wanted to hug me. No longer interested in finishing the conversation, I turned back to say goodbye to Phil and Macy. Barbara turned to them and began 'Isn't she just the most incred…' Phil finished her sentence 'Incredibly beautiful, yeah, great to meet you, Alice'.

We got in to the convertible and drove to the most magical home in the hills and in a short space of time the journey to Rome was lost in the view. I bathed and slept and swam and ate and talked and laughed through tired eyes as two nights and a day went by in a bubble of comfort.

Bagno Vignoni - Radicofani. September

Barbara drove me until we found a Via Francigena sign. I was back on my journey and she returned to hers. I knew this was the final push. I had allocated eight days for the rest of the way and given Muma a date and time for my arrival in St Peter's Square. I would have no more days off and even though I had the itinerary down on paper, arriving in St Peter's on the morning of the first of October, I still could not make myself believe it or feel any excitement about it.

I knew I had to make it in order to move on to the next stage in life confident rather than defeated. For the first time ever I want to live, I want to pursue a life that develops the fulfillment of my soul and I no longer feel the pull of suicide. First I have to complete the trial I have set myself which will form a foundation and reference for the future.

My feet hurt and hurt and having spent most of the last twenty-four hours asleep I was longing to sleep again. There was something still in the atmosphere today. The sun seemed as if it might set in the East. It gave off a low pale light all day and not much heat despite few clouds. I passed two sheepdogs sitting at a road end, leaning against each other and looking out at the view. They didn't even flinch as I passed. I stood and watched two horses standing on a mound, head to tail, touching at the widest part of their bulging bodies, just looking out at the vast views North and South. I ate peaches and chocolate as the farmer ploughed and I headed for the flat top mountain where Radicofani nestled into the other side.

The stone is grey and pale and there are few people about. The narrow streets are steep and the view falls away in the distance as you look down them. On the church door was a list of three telephone numbers for pilgrims. I called the first one and got the answering machine. I tried the next one and a man answered 'Pronto'. I spoke in English but got no response so proceeded to read out the title of the notice on the church door 'Pellegrini Chiesa di San Pietro'. This was enough for him to understand me and after his 'sì' I waited for him hopefully.

I spent five minutes slumped on the steps of the church before a little old woman turned up. She had a smile in competition with mine. We shook hands and went through a door opposite the church and up some stone stairs into a shiny clean hostel with a kitchen, a long table in the hall and three rooms with several bunks to choose from. I showered and got into bed and slept for four hours. Thankfully the unbearable heat of the summer has gone. It is now much cooler and easier for both walking and sleeping.

I found a small food shop tucked away in what the owner described as the square of paradise. I must have talked to her for half an hour.

She was desperate that we should understand each other. We scribbled on paper for wrapping bread: names, dates, ages and pictures. I told her where I was from and what I was doing. She told me her son is 33 tomorrow, twenty-four pilgrims were in her shop yesterday, the cheese is from sheep and Aquapentente, the place I was headed tomorrow, is downhill and up. I thought I understood her but her shop was tiny and I cannot believe that in one day she saw more than double the amount of pilgrims I have seen in two and half months. We kissed goodbye and I went back to the hostel with bags of food.

A German man and his mother have arrived. They are doing a bus-and-walking trip to Rome and are pretty friendly considering they are German. It is difficult for the mother, as she does not speak a word of English, but the son, although camp, is a nice guy. They would have asked me to eat with them but I was in bed long before they headed out.

It was at this stage in the journey that I needed books the most. I read whenever I found myself alone and not walking. It was wonderful to live in another mind and escape my own thoughts. I had no patience left for the remaining seven days. If I could polish them off in one go, I would, but the thought of splitting them into seven sections, getting through each one individually but with exactly the same routine, weighed me down like a gas balloon tied to the ground.

Radicofani - Acquapendente. September

I woke early and left Radicofani via Paradise Square to give Silvia two kisses. She was receiving the bread delivery and was already stuck in to a new day. I walked for two hours along a ridge with shooting down both sides. The sun was barely up but I was far from alone. I passed a parked car with a man fast asleep in the back and found myself almost tiptoeing past for fear of waking him. I crossed the border into Lazio, the final region of my journey, and stopped for coffee and a dried out pastry in a down-and-out roadside café. A young girl was helping her mother behind the bar. There were several men in camouflage drinking coffee standing up and looking at me from the floor upwards. I paid the young girl and she smiled and winked in a way far too advanced for her age.

I left the roadside to climb back up onto dusty tracks. Although I felt vulnerable on them they offered a much softer surface for my sore soles. A Land Rover full of men with guns slowed up when it went past me and the driver hung out of his window with a smirk and eyes as if to say I could have you if I really wanted. I hate it, I hate the fact you cannot smile and say hello in a genuinely friendly way. If I was to give an inch they would stop and I would be in their control. Instead I glance at them with a confidence to say I am wrapped up in my own world and you ain't going to get any more attention. I really dislike doing it.

There are some wonderful things to see in Italy so, unlike to the Alps, I would not mind returning, but only with someone else. It is not a country that draws you to uncover its heart and soul because it does not have a nice feeling and there is something odd about the people. There are some dark undercurrents. I rarely see a woman and never far from her house whereas men are everywhere, on the street, in the woods, far down isolated dusty tracks, and they have such a horrible look in their eye. They gamble, they drink, and they stare from toe to breast. I am so ready to get out of here.

Having descended from Radicofani I stopped in Proceno for a can of coke before the steep climb to Aquapendente. I sat outside the café and a man who had been watching me from the square opposite came over and sat in a plastic chair behind me. 'Do you want some wine?' he asked as he held the bottle at an angle displaying it to me. 'I don't think it would help me,' I replied smiling at him. 'Yes, it would.' 'No, thank you' I began to put my boots back on, turning away from him. The bottle hit the ground as if it should have broken. 'Are you leaving me?' 'I've got to keep going'. 'Where are you going?' 'Aquapendente.' 'I drive you.' He got up. 'My car is round the corner'. 'No, thank you, I must walk'. He stumbled into my chair as I pushed it out behind me and fell backwards into his plastic seat to drool at the pavement.

La Casa del Pellegrino has a sad crumbling stone façade. There were three telephone numbers pinned to the door. Having got an answer from none of them I went round the corner to look at the cathedral. I saw an old woman looking down at the street below from a window high up. I hoped she might help me but my smile of 'buongiorno' sent her retreating back into a dark room. I tried one of the numbers again and spoke some half Italian down the line. Five minutes later a woman turned up and let me in. It's cold, dark and dirty. I chose one of three rooms with a double bed. As the boiler was heating the water in the bathroom the two Germans I met last night turned up together with an elderly good-looking German couple. The camp son was taken aback by the grottiness of the hostel. He stood with soft legs as though, if he stood up straight, the ceiling might spoil his hair-do. He smiled as though he had a lisp. His mother had the most bad-tempered expression that, owing to her heavily hooded eyes, does not soften when she smiled. They didn't stay long and left to find somewhere with less damp in the air. The other couple were taken up with unpacking their panniers and getting their room in order before I had a chance to say hello. She was so preoccupied with looking in every room and cupboard that my attempt to chitchat was brushed aside. The man is a beanpole, his tight cycling shorts are baggy round his wrinkly thighs and he appears to have had a facelift. He stood tall in the dark kitchen letting the woman with him flurry her feathers before he could find his place. I jumped into conversation as an excuse to stare at his amazing bone structure and old yet smooth skin. He found himself very funny and with his face scrunched up in silent laughter he lost his looks. He joked about the fact he could not see my halo and I told him it still had a few days to arrive. The woman had now slowed down a bit and he headed to join her in their room.

I showered and went to find some food in the town. It was a very peculiar place. The people looked at me as if I had lost my way and really should not be here. The choice of food was poor. Every shop had the same selection of warm refrigerators, dusty packets and bruised fruit and veg. In one shop a woman tried to give me a basket. I attempted to tell her I was just looking but she held me firmly by the arm insisting I took the basket from her. I shrugged free and said 'non' and left with a huff from her. I returned to the hostel with two soft tomatoes, two bread rolls and a slice of take-away pizza. The others had gone out and I was asleep by seven.

Acquapendente - Bolsena. September

The mist was so thick I could barely see the road in front of me. The air was cold and the sunlight could hardly get through. I left Aquapentente on the main road, afraid of drivers not being able to see me. I walked fast, bathed in a mystical light, barely able to see my own feet as I searched for a track through the fields. When I turned off the road the weightless mist was still consuming me in silence. I was the only person around and the cobwebs glistened in the morning dew. It was hauntingly beautiful. I climbed uphill to San Lorenzo Nuovo and stopped for coffee in a café overlooking the main square. The mist had dispersed and the clouds floated up giving a clear view down on Lago di Bolsena as I exited the town. Looking out over fertile land that sloped all the way down to the banks of the huge glistening volcanic lake made me desperately want to be in it.

I daydreamed of swimming and my feet carried me right to the shore of the lake, way off the direct route to Bolsena where I was planning to spend the night. There was a large stiff serpent of a sewage pipe stretching into the lake. With not enough of a beach to walk along the shore I headed back to the main road. I passed several roads down to the lake but they all had iron gates with Private signs and I did not want to bait a short-tempered Italian. The next track I came to went straight to the water's edge. There was a small pebbly jut but it had a rotting bird splayed on it, which put me off. I gave up on the thought of swimming and trod the main road to Bolsena. My feet were so sore by the time I arrived but my rekindled desperation to be in the water led me away from the town and down to the lakeshore. There was a marina with a gravel beach to one side. Several people sat in the café behind but no one was swimming under the cloudy sky. I laid down my stick, took off my rucksack and changed into my swimming costume with as much modesty as possible on a patch of grass between the café and the water.

Savoring every moment, I walked towards the water, feeling it already in contact with my body. To float in something completely natural in a weightless, gravity-less state is total pleasure. I lay on my back and looked up at the sky consumed with the feeling of pure happiness. With not a care for anyone around, I kicked my legs furiously like a frustrated child throwing a tantrum. It did wonders for my numb soles. Chilled by the increasingly grey sky I went to find a bed for the night.

I have found my way to a convent next to La Basilica di Santa Cristina. A black nun let me in and showed me to a clean bedroom with two beds and a bathroom. No sooner had I washed and got into bed than the German mother and son turned up. She settled on the bed next to me and he pulled out a camp bed in the corridor. The mother now likes to talk at me in German as if I understand. When she went for a shower I remained in bed and talked to the son. He is very nice and as they are heading to Rome tomorrow he gave me his maps for the final six days I had ahead. It was very kind of him and I was particularly pleased to have a map for walking into Rome as this was the one day I did not want to get lost.

After we had all lounged around in our room long enough the mother and son went off to walk down to the lake and I crossed the square into la Basilica di Santa Cristina, a huge church at the southern end of this small town. It was founded in the 11th century nearby the tomb of Santa Cristina, a saint from the 3rd century whose legend suggests that the young daughter of a rich magistrate was converted to Christianity against her father's will. She was punished for destroying her father's pagan idols and the tortures she suffered at first left no trace but as they became more severe so she died. The original structure was erected in honour of Santa Cristina; however, a miraculous event occurred here in 1263 and so the building was developed in the 13th century and onwards into the 15th century.

Bolsena was a major town on the pilgrims route to Rome and one priest on his way to Rome in 1263 stopped to pray at Santa Cristina's tomb. His faith was wavering and as he celebrated the Eucharist by her tomb he asked for the Saint to intervene and strengthen his faith. At the moment of consecration, as he held the host in the air, blood began to ooze from it. Moved by what was happening the priest made his way with the Eucharist wrapped in linen to the sacristy and on the way a few drops of blood fell on the marble floor. In 1963 a baroque chapel dedicated to the miracle was built alongside the main basilica. Today this chapel houses the altar at which the priest said Mass and the bloodstained slabs of marble framed within a gold chest. Once seen, it is hard not to believe this story.

People were filling up the pews for Mass so I joined them for a rather long service during which two things amused me; a tone-deaf nun who, plugged into a loud speaker, lead the singing with totally uninhibited enthusiasm, and a busybody. The busybody sat at the front of the church endlessly turning round to survey the congregation and nod at familiar faces. When it came to the collection she rose from her pew like a swelling marshmallow and stood facing the altar carrying her great weight on quivering high heels. Her cellulite thighs were shown off in a pair of shocking pink leggings pulled up into the crack of her bottom. As she bowed to the altar her saggy bottom gave a vertical smile to the congregation before she turned and waddled, head held high, unstably up the aisle in her patent high heels. Her whole demeanour was so out of kilter with the mindset of the devout observers that it made me smile a lot.

Bolsena - Montefiascone. September

After breakfast in the convent with the Germans I climbed up above Lago di Bolsena to the hill top town of Montefiasconi. At 633 metres there was no higher hill to be climbed between here and Rome. For the past week I have been entering and leaving towns through wonderful Roman arches and it feels like I am on a straight path to St Peter's. Montefiasconi was no exception. It is a medieval town perched above Lake Bolsena to the North, the plains of Viterbo to the South, and its skyline is dominated by the huge Dome of la Cattedrale di Santa Margherita, one of the largest domes in Italy.

I am staying in another convent although this one was rather harder to get into. It had no obvious entrance and no buzzer on the vaguely suitable door. I walked all the way round its walls, which took me back onto the road skirting the city walls. I re-entered the main city gate as if entering the town for the first time and went back to the only door of the convent. I tried the handle and in I went to a dark porch with a big wooden door and a buzzer by the side. I pressed the button and the door opened onto a long vaulted stone corridor. To the right was a small room with a miniature nun sitting behind an empty desk. She stood up, gaining little height, and led me up the corridor and on up a flight of stone steps onto an equally long and dark corridor. As she did her wimple billowed off her shoulders in a non-existent breeze. I looked straight at her feet to make sure she wasn't floating. There was something very eerie about this place.

She let me into a room of five beds all with wrinkled bottom sheets. The bathroom minus a loo seat was absolutely filthy. The drain in the middle of the floor was so clogged up with hair it looked like a dead weed in a flowerbed of tiles. I seriously considered not washing but my own smell got the better of me. I had sweated more than usual today due to coming face to face with two very large wild boar in a wood. I had heard a rustling ahead of me but didn't even consider it would be wild boar. Suddenly we were staring at each other with very little space between us. I raised my stick and shouted 'Arghh' at the top of my voice for as long as it took them to run off in the opposite direction. I then walked as fast as I possibly could uphill on a steep track through the wood, out of breath and pouring with sweat. I showered and knew this room with no crucifix was going to frighten me if I spent too much time in it, so I went out to lunch in the only restaurant open on a Monday.

I have come into a large room with three other people, two women eating together and a man alone. I asked for a table for one and the stereotypical Italian waiter-cum-chef swayed his hand out across the whole room. There were two small tables: one snug next to the single man and one by the draughty entrance, awkwardly sectioned off from the door with a Chinese blind. I went and sat at the table by the door, feeling almost as awkward as I would have been sitting next to the man, and randomly picked something to eat from an unintelligible menu. It was filthy. Gnocci were followed by chicken in a rich creamy sauce that set as it got cold.

The sun was out and I walked up to the park with my book. The only other person there was a grubby-looking man with tattoos and a lip piercing. He was holding his violent-eyed Rottweiler with one hand on the lead close to its collar and the other with the lead wound round his fist so as to gain enough control to pull against the strength of the dog. I quickly found my way back out of the park and instead sat on a bench in the hot sun facing the scaffolding-covered Cathedral. To begin with, despite the heat of the sun, it was peaceful. But then I realised, looking up into the scaffolding, the workmen were standing in a line just watching me. Once I had seen them they got back to work and the crashing and drilling was too much so I went back to my room.

That night I slept so badly. I tried not to but I felt spooked in my room. I kept getting up and wandering round it to maintain confidence in the whole space but it was so large and dark that each time I did it I had to turn on the overhead lights (there is never a sidelight in pilgrim dorms) and when I turned them off again it was such a contrast and so dark I immediately felt frightened again. I am also unable to sleep with the window closed but this being a hill top town the wind howled and howled, sounding as if it was trying to say something, which didn't help.

Montefiascone - Vetralla. September

I got up at six-thirty and by quarter to seven I had felt my way down the long dark corridor to the huge wooden entrance door. I could not find a light switch but knew the latch on the door and could picture the freedom of the street on the other side. As I was feeling for the lock I felt my way along a huge bolt which, much as I tried, I could not budge. I walked back up the corridor towards the stairs if only to get some light. At a right angle to the stairs was a dully-lit corridor into the convent. As if on cue a black nun in a white habit came rushing down with the sound of jangling keys. She hurried to the front door and unlocked it, with both of us standing side by side unable to communicate in the dark. I stepped out into a wind howling down the street. Shutters were banging, plastic bottles were tumbling over the cobbles and the darkness of winter was beginning to settle in.

This morning I had got dressed over my swimming costume in the knowledge that I would be walking past the uncommercial thermal ponds of Bagnaccio. There was no missing them with the smell of sulphur getting stronger the closer I got. In the middle of farmland was a small fenced-off area with several campervans parked by a network of thermal springs. It was eight-thirty and there were already several old age pensioners in swimming costumes sitting in the pool with their feet floating to the surface. I stripped off right by the side and hopped in amongst the solid round tummies and wrinkly-armed Italians. Apart from an exchange of 'buongiorno' not one of them took any notice of me until it was time to change awkwardly on a bench nearby and then they all stared at my great effort to get out of my wet swimming costume, dry off with a very small towel and put on my shorts and t-shirt.

Viterbo was the last big city I had to pass through before Rome. I am not a city person and I was keen to get on through it and stay somewhere smaller but first I took a detour through the historic gently ascending narrow streets to Piazza San Lorenzo. Across one end of the square stretches the Palazzo dei Papi built between 1255 and 1267 to house various Popes who sought refuge in Viterbo during a turbulent political time in Rome. It is an elegant gothic building part of which forms an open-top colonnaded bridge down to the lower levels of the city walls. The Papal Palace is well known for being the place of the longest ever conclave which began in 1268 and continued for almost three years, for a year and a half of which the undecided Cardinals were locked into a room and rationed on bread and water. With help from the locals, who broke in through the roof to nourish the Cardinals, the meeting continued for almost another year before Pope Gregory X was finally—but not totally unanimously—elected

Pope. The Cattedrale di San Lorenzo to the side of the palace and the centre of the south side of the square is a weighty, simple structure and surprisingly modest inside perhaps due to the heavy bombing Viterbo suffered during World War II. Within the bare space there is an eye-catching decorative mosaic marble floor and beautiful naïve medieval carvings on the capitals.

The museum shop by the side of the cathedral had a Via Francigena sign in the window so I went to ask about accommodation outside the city. There, talking to the man behind the counter, was the German man with the face-lift. He turned round to leave and I said 'hello'. He smiled until his face was tight shut repeating my name over and over again, 'Alise, Alise, Alise'. He then practically jumped with excitement as he told me about the famously long papal election. His English was good enough for me to understand but not good enough to have a conversation so I just let him go on. After we had finished trying to understand each other and I had spent ten minutes hopping from sore sole to sore sole longing to take my rucksack off, I had missed my place in the queue. When it eventually came to my turn the man was no help at all. He had a wall of computers behind him but refused to look online and see if there was accommodation for me in the next town, Vetralla. If I were to stay in Viterbo it would have made the next two days very long whereas if I pushed on today I would then even up the distance to Rome. He told me there was no pilgrim accommodation in Vetralla but something in me did not believe him so I decided to keep going and left with that horrible uncertainty of heading somewhere I had been told there was nowhere to stay.

I walked along a track parallel to the barriers of a motorway. The road was heavy with traffic and the noise rattled my head. The sulphurous water of the thermal pools had softened my feet, which added to the pain and having taken ibuprofen on little food my tummy was in turmoil. There was nothing to go to the loo behind so crouching as close to the barrier as I could I just had to give in to the humiliation and hope the traffic was going fast enough not to notice me. Afterwards I was very hungry so I stopped under a road traversing the motorway and ate every bit of food I had. I knew it was a foolish thing to do with a long way to go and no guarantee of anything to eat at the other end but by this stage of what was now an enormous struggle I got a kick out of going against rational thought.

I left the side of the motorway and trying to shorten the distance I joined what I had not realised was a very busy road. The maps the German boy had given me were out of date and the small-looking road had become much larger and rather dangerous for walking. However if I went along it for one junction I cut four kilometres off my forty-kilometre day. This was definitely worth it.

It is always baking hot walking on a main road with no shade and heavy traffic but the endless friendly tooting made me smile a lot. I saw a small white car pull over ahead of me. As I approached it on the other side of the road, a man got out and shouted 'Pellegrino?', 'Sì' I shouted back. He then shouted something I didn't understand so with a gap in the traffic I crossed over. I saw he was wearing a dog collar, and so acute were my senses at first I thought it might be a particularly dark way of picking up solo girls but I was soon reassured. As we stood making no sense to each other four children clambered like monkeys out of the car and stood close to the priest with their eyes glued to me. I told him I was heading for Vetralla and he kept repeating San Francesco, San Francesco. They all got back in the car and I crossed the road and waved as he tooted his horn.

Vetralla is another historic town on a small hill. It seems a poor place with few people about. I could not see a church so I went in to the town hall and smiled at a woman and said 'San Francesco?' She walked me outside and pointed on down the main street. My feet were agony so before going any further I rested in a café eating ice cream and drinking fizzy water.

Having mustered a little more strength I went on down the main street at the end of which was the church of San Francesco. Nearby I went under an arch into a playground of energetic children. A short shaven-headed man came up to me with a broad grin of welcome. He led me up some metal stairs into a room with many more children sitting in groups round a big u-shape of tables, scribbling in colouring books. Towering over them was the priest whom I had met on the road. He crossed the room and shook my hand and that was about the extent of any more communication we had. The petite man with an enormous cross round his neck whose demeanour suggested an Opus Dei follower laid me a place on an empty table. I sat down as bread and fried pasta and two chunks of mashed together meat in tomato sauce were put in front of me. I sensed the priest was telling the children about me and one little boy rushed towards me and pushed himself up on his tiptoes to give me a kiss. I ate as if I was hungry and the children swivelled in their chairs smiling at me. I finished and took my plastic plates into the room they had come out of, a tiny kitchen with no one in it. I sat back down at the table so relieved to have the pressure off my soles.

The man who seemed to make me his duty reappeared and asked 'You want to stay?' 'Sì' I replied. He led me across the playground, down into a damp basement and opened the door to a room with three beds, all with stained mattresses. He then pointed at a door across the alley of the basement and said 'bathroom'. There was one more door, which was his room. His English was minimal and when he left my room he said 'hello'. He came back to tell me dinner was at seven and then left saying 'hello' again. It was so funny when it happened I had to try hard not to laugh out loud.

The bathroom is even dirtier than yesterday's. It really is the filthiest I have seen. I showered with my shoes right by the curtain so as to avoid any direct contact with the floor. My room is almost as bad except it is dry. I lay on the bed trying to get the feeling back into my feet. The soles are completely numb and have felt that way for the last two days. Little did I know just how much rest it would take to get any feeling back in to them.

At six-thirty my little leader knocked on the door and we went upstairs to sit on a bench overlooking the now empty playground. A short Italian man covered in tattoos hobbled towards us. He had broken his coccyx and carried a fat wooden stick with a scull carved on top. He sat down on my other side and all three of us were now rather close. He showed me his knuckles, fist scrunched up. They had the letters H A T E tattooed across them. 'It's English. You understand' he said as his eyes sparkled. His English was good but only when he wanted to say something. 'You believe in Jesus' he asked in a firm tone. I was far too taken aback with fear to say anything other than 'Yes'. His name was Giorgio and the other man who is Hungarian is called Jan. Giorgio, so as to keep conversation going, was ordered by Jan to sit with us while we ate more pasta and mushed-up meat in an empty room. They were both intimidating, threatening characters although sweet and helpless at the same time. Jan hardly ate a thing and I had to plough through my full plate at great speed so as to keep up with him. With translation by Giorgio they talked only about women. My mind drifted to the bedroom with no lock on the door and I stood up and told them I must sleep. They said we could all have coffee at seven o'clock tomorrow morning.

Vetralla - Sutri. September

After a cup of thick sugary coffee with Giorgio and Jan they gave me a bag of bruised fruit and I was off. In four days time I would be arriving in Rome but still I could not get my head round the fact it was actually going to happen and the distance each day continued to weigh my sore feet down as I alternated paracetamol and ibuprofen. My mind is running out of patience for my own company and I am incredibly lonely. I so hope I will never have a period in life ahead when I identify with these feelings.

The mental struggle of doubting that I would make it was so consuming that both finding a bed for the night and concentrating on where I was going hardly entered my thoughts. I headed off with a carefree swagger in what I sensed was the direction of Rome, this occasionally confirmed by irregular Via Francigena signs. I had got used to the abrupt Italian manner and was no longer worried about not speaking the language. The only thing that made me nervous was the thought of the big roads on the way into Rome.

I had left Vetralla and was heading up a narrow country lane longing to pass through a village for breakfast. Up in front of me were two men in brand new walking kit. Matching bags, clean boots, Quencha clothing and sharp points on their walking poles. They were standing at a crossroads looking at their map. I walked quickly to catch them up and on reaching them I asked if they spoke English. They both turned their eyes up from the map, one looking out over the bridge of his glasses and said 'yes'. Checking in my guidebook I told them the route was straight on. They smiled and strode on with an air of nervousness about the day ahead. I kept up with them for a bit but their quick pace and lack of chat sent me on a detour to a nearby village to find something to eat.

As I was re-joining the route I coincided with a group of eleven pilgrims all eager to shake my hand and beam with enthusiasm that we were all in it together. They had walked from Aquapendente and were full of the joys of being a pilgrim. In the space of an hour I had seen more pilgrims than I had seen in nearly three months. I was full of enthusiasm for meeting them but inside I had a mental battle going on which was subdued by their upbeat energy which I could not siphon off.

I walked with a man, Alberto, who spoke good English. He was very interested in the analytical detail of my walk, the signs, the accommodation, and the safety. He then told me that he had created a job for himself by raising awareness of the Via Francigena. He had organised the group and they were walking ten days of the final region to Rome. Everything was recorded through a GPS transmitter in his rucksack, someone had a video camera and many people were taking photographs. I told him that for me I had only got as far as I had by believing in God. I then asked if he was a Catholic. He was an agnostic, which led me inquisitively into what it was that drove him to do pilgrimages. He talked of the geography, travelling, organising groups and enjoying walking but nothing he said touched any of the depth I had found. My approach to the journey has made it far more mentally challenging than physically but overall this has made it hugely uplifting from deep down inside. I asked if he felt anything spiritual or religious about the walk and he replied that it was a challenge to remain agnostic doing it but that he did.

His eyes darted around never looking at me in a settled way. There was something unusual about Alberto and I could not work it out until he began to describe his house. He told me he lived in Roppollo and started going into detail about the labyrinth in his garden. I tapped him on the shoulder and said 'I have been to your house'. He looked at me dead straight with wide-open eyes as I said 'I stayed there when Carla was housesitting'. He could not believe it and announced to the group that I had stayed in his house while he was away on holiday. It was a bizarre coincidence but for me this unsettled man and peculiar house now both made sense.

Having met online, they were a motley crew of all ages but very friendly and almost immediately they wanted to include me in where they were staying and travel the rest of the journey together. I told them today I was going to Sutri and they said there was nowhere to stay in Sutri but that I could get a lift with them to a nearby hostel. I did not want to make any set plans and thanked them without saying yes. We all walked together for at least two hours; however, they moved in contraction, like a snake eating a mouse, as the group strung out and came together. This involved many stops, which made it a lethargic process, so at stop number three I left them to rest and continued alone through the hazel groves.

I stopped for a sandwich in a roadside café under the walls of Capranica and as I got up to leave I saw the two Italian men eating lunch high up on the wall. I called up to them and they waved and said they would be down in five minutes. I got an apple out of my bag and sat on a crumbling wall waiting for them. It was only five more kilometres to Sutri and with most of the day over the men were relaxed and far more forthcoming.

Cristian and Claudio are the oldest and youngest of four brothers and having never walked before they have set themselves the challenge of walking to Rome from Viterbo. Their first day was yesterday and they were shocked by what hard work walking becomes if you do it hour after hour. We talked in English the whole way to Sutri and I enjoyed their company so much. They had organised their journey thoroughly and had pre-booked into a convent for tonight. On hearing

I had made no plans they both took responsibility and said they would definitely get me a bed in the convent too.

We climbed up to the historic town of Sutri which perches up on a rocky hill. When we reached the convent there was a notice on the door telling pilgrims to come at three-fifteen and it was only two o'clock. We walked along the main street of this ancient small town to have a look at the cathedral. The men genuflected and made the sign of the cross and I conceitedly thought I could have guessed they were Catholics. La Cattedrale di Santa Maria Assunta was founded in the 12th century on the site of a much older Roman temple. Though heavily restored, the original Romanesque crypt remains intact. We followed each other down beneath the altar into a large space with eight small naves and a central apse resting on reused Roman columns whose capitals were carved with foliage.

Afterwards we sat outside a café eating ice cream, looking at photographs of their respective families and kicking around time until three-fifteen when we went to ring the buzzer of the convent. Thank goodness I was with Italians. The convent is the order of Carmelite nuns in which silence is sacred and communication is limited. We waited enclosed in a dark hall opposite a wooden box similar to a confessional. Eventually after I entertained myself imagining that something totally unexpected might happen, a light was put on behind the lattice grill and a timid nun spoke with the brothers. We placed our passports and twenty euros each into a revolving hatch and back came three keys. Down the street we let ourselves in through a door to a steep set of stairs and a corridor with rooms off it. For the first time on all of this journey I did not say a word and got a room all to myself. I had clean sheets, my own bathroom and a desk to write at, I was so happy.

I slept and wandered into town to buy some food. Back in my room I washed my clothes and as I was hanging them out of the window I saw the grinning German bicyclist below. I could not believe it. There he was like a lost pop-up character. 'Hey' I said. 'Alise, Alise, Alise!' he exclaimed full of excitement. I went downstairs and let him in. He fumbled a key in his hands, unable to read the number without his glasses. I took it from him and led him to his room, asking him how it was possible that we moved at the same speed despite his being on a bicycle. He told me his girlfriend was writing a guidebook and therefore they moved slowly. I went into his room curious to have a snoop around and, reassured by the fact he was an old man and had a girlfriend, I enjoyed grinning at him with flirtatious enthusiasm, which gave him such pleasure. He kindly suggested I join them for dinner but I said I must sleep and without any explanation I bore the brunt of his joking about how much sleeping I do.

Ten minutes later Cristian knocked on my door to say they would go for dinner at seven-thirty. I told him I must sleep and that I would see them tomorrow. They were leaving far earlier than I was but he kindly said he would book me into where they were staying tomorrow in Campagnano di Roma. What a joy it was to have met two inclusive, genuine, helpful Italian men with no ulterior motive. It really felt as if they had been sent from heaven.

Sutri – Campagnano di Roma. September

It was cold when I stepped outside but the baker was just opening her doors and the apple pastries were piping hot and warmed me up as I ate them in the small main square, perched up against the central fountain listening to the ringing bells above the Etruscan-Roman arch. Sutri's ancient Etruscan origins became even clearer as I left the town down through the archaeological park below. Lazio is a volcanic region where the hills of the landscape are more often than not caldera, ridges of volcanic craters made of tufa. Around Sutri the Etruscans took advantage of elements of this rock formed through years of compressed volcanic ash and excavated tombs and a modest Amphitheatre. I must have walked past over 60 graves of the necropolis dug into the rock as I entered the grass oval of the Amphitheatre. It was entirely carved out of the rock and much smaller than that of Rome, but once inside it contained the same hostile air of a place where two people fighting to death was a spectator sport.

An hour into the day I was completely lost. My directions said turn left at the T-junction but the track I was on faded out and there was no obvious junction. I tried turning left but the wood was so thick I knew it couldn't possibly be right. I followed the track back a little way but couldn't find it. I could hear a main road across the fields to my left so I decided to head towards it and hope to follow it to the next town. I went in a diagonal across a large muddy field towards a house, hoping that I could join the drive and reach the main road. I was way off my map and so lonely I felt like bursting into tears. As I walked through the garden of the house a collie dog came bounding towards me barking like crazy. Much to my relief no one came out and I headed for the drive as fast as I could. The dog ran circles around me barking ferociously and jumping up with a snapping mouth. Thankfully my rucksack overhung my bottom so he bit it instead. I was nervous of the dog but I was far more frightened by the possibility of its owner being alerted and my having to face the wrath of an Italian farmer. This gave me determination to continue down the drive despite the dog's insane gymnastics. When I was far enough away from the house I beat the dog. This was a bad idea. It became crosser and consequently I had to thrash my stick violently in front of me to keep it away. At the end of the drive I could see two huge solid metal gates set between a high brick wall. I went to it praying the gates would open. They were bolted shut with a heavy padlock but there was a slim gap between the wall and the gate, filled with strips of barbed wire. On the other side there was a very fast main road with no verge. The dog bared his teeth at me and I knew I had no time to hang about. With calm speed I untangled a big enough hole and pushing my bag through first I gave the dog one final whack with my stick and as it whimpered backwards dragging its behind I tunnelled myself headfirst through the gap in the wire. I re-tangled it across the hole as the traffic sped past.

I felt as if I had jumped from one death camp into another. The road was narrow with no verge and the drivers fled past at reckless speed. I walked against the traffic until I came to a track and thought better to be lost in the fields than killed on the road so headed down it. I saw a farmer rounding up his sheep and knowing he had seen me I headed straight towards him. I pointed at a village on my map and he just glared at me paying no attention to my finger. He said absolutely nothing so I carried on with confidence across the field hoping to re-find my path. I came to a stream and followed it for an hour before a path appeared on the other side and I knew where I was. I had walked for two hours but had only gone five kilometres of the official route. Fed up I lay down in the grass and ate a banana, becoming more determined to pay attention when I continued.

An hour and a half later I entered Monterosi where I refuelled on coffee and apricot tart. Campagnano di Roma was another sixteen kilometres further on and the thought of over three hours more of walking filled me with dread. I left the café angry with my feet whose pain never subsides. Away from the town and down a dry crumbly track I caught up with Cristian and Claudio. I was so pleased to see them. We walked on together and ploughed through the kilometres with upbeat conversation. At Cascate Monte Gelato on the river Treja we stopped to cool our feet in the burbling stream. The brothers offered to share their lunch but I pushed on, desperate to reach the end of the day's walking. As if from nowhere the German bicyclist and his preoccupied girlfriend came up behind me. She hovered around taking photographs as he stood and talked rather too close to me. Dressed in lycra shorts and no t-shirt his willy was an embarrassingly obvious bulge in his shorts and together with his pulled-up ankle socks and plastic crocs he really was quite a sight.

Leaving me behind in their tyre marks, I plugged into my i-pod to drown out the pain of my swollen feet before I met the Germans again pushing their way up the rocky slope into Campagnano di Roma. From across the main square I heard voices shouting my name. There were the eleven enthusiastic pilgrims sitting round a table of empty beer bottles. I went and joined them until the Italian brothers arrived. As soon as they did we left in search of ice cream. The group was going on to the next town for the night and the bicyclists had pedalled on through. There was no way I could have made it any further today and what luck I had Cristian and Claudio's company to enjoy and keep my depression at bay.

We sat shoulder to shoulder on the pavement outside a bar indulging in overflowing pots of ice-cold sweet ice cream. Three passers-by engaged me in conversation. They were young men researching the Via Francigena for a pre-planned three-day walk to Rome. They asked where I had walked from and when I told them they were speechless and just stood on the pavement not wanting to leave. It was mildly embarrassing.

Cristian and Claudio had pre-arranged to meet under the stone arch, Porta di Roma, at the South of the town, a man who was going to take us to the local community centre. There he was sitting in his red shirt. We followed him as he led with shoulders slumped forward, arms rigidly straight and palms facing backwards. Down a street, round a corner, down another street and round several more corners we went as he stopped to say hello to every bar tender, garage mechanic and street sweeper we past. He led us up the stairs to the top floor of the community centre where there was a long attic full of mattresses. We then had to go back downstairs to get our pilgrim passports stamped. As all three of us crammed into a tiny office another man appeared. He looked at me and saying something in Italian led me to a room down the corridor with one mattress in it. Back upstairs to pick up my rucksack the brothers were amused by the fact the Italian man had looked at me and said 'you need privacy'. We all agreed a time to meet for dinner and I asked if they would knock on my door and wake me up ten minutes before. On the way downstairs I met a tall man. He said 'you must be Alice from Scotland'. He had heard about me from Marinka and Evert and had been one day behind me for the last month. There was a Swiss coolness about him but he was good-looking for an old man. I suggested he join us for dinner and so he did.

After a knock on my door I pulled myself up for dinner and we all went to a bar for a drink. It was full of men and later in the restaurant I was also in the minority. However I was so pleased to have found two Italians who did not stare with predatory eyes and instead offered such good company. I felt exhausted and dipped in and out of conversation until the Swiss man started a heated debate. He began by saying that to be gay is normal. He then went on to criticise the Catholic Church for being full of gays. When he got on to saying it is also full of paedophiles my heartbeat tripled to the metre of the syllables but without a drink inside me I was able discuss it without being too forceful or irrational. Having agreed that the Catholic Church is a focused minority in a worldwide issue, he became keener on repeating the fact that being gay was normal. His whole theory that being gay is normal—somehow reinforced by the fact that his children's guinea-pigs were gay—became flawed when we got on to talking about his possible reaction should his seven-year-old son come home and say that he was in love with his best friend John. Would he treat this as completely normal or would they discuss it as a possible complication? I said that the Catholic Church sets an example, like parents in a family, and that—even if one had not always lived by the example—it is important for parents to set it. Without an example direction is lost and more often than not children become damaged by the consequences. Cristian and Claudio were far too accepting to voice their opinion so I did not write off the Swiss man completely.

Campagnano di Roma - Ottavia. September

Staying up for dinner last night was a mistake. I was not in my sleeping bag on the floor until 10pm and I woke this morning with a headache, which I battled against all day. In company my head lets me down and I struggle to keep up mentally which wears me out so much more than the physical side of walking. I set off after the others but soon caught up after walking at great speed having frightened myself. I really do not like snakes but masochistically longed to see one. This morning I saw the longest fattest bright green snake I have ever seen and it frightened me into a quick pace.

Although we were close to Rome the route, which crossed the Parco Naturale di Velo, was surprisingly rural, on farm and woodland tracks for most of the day. It is the second last day of the whole journey and they say you get reluctant to finish the closer you get to Rome but I could not wait to have arrived in St Peter's Square and get on and live life. We walked as a four but as I tried to find common ground with the Swiss man so the gap widened between the brothers and us. When we reached Formello the Swiss was determined to follow his map round the outskirts for fear of getting lost so I left him and entered the historic town through a Roman arch. A woman on the street asked me if I was a pilgrim. I held her shoulder and with a huge grin I told her I was a pilgrim for one more day. On hearing where I had started she asked me to come to her office to do an interview for the local paper. I gave her my number and said until it is over I can give you very few answers. I breathed in the smell of fresh flowers in a church and on leaving the town I saw the brothers up ahead of me. I called to them and with broad smiles they waited for me to catch up. I was exhausted and my head so sore that I was reliant on their company to keep me going. Thank goodness I had met them.

As we approached Rome the roads got bigger. The charms of the journey had gone and instead we were joining the cars on a very busy highway. Gone is the silence and instead you feel you are being kicked aside by modern transport. We walked in single file and two protective gentlemen guarded me in the middle. When we joined the stretch of main road that would take us into Rome the following day we crossed paths with the two German bicyclists. It was yet another hilarious coincidence. We all kissed goodbye and waved them on up the road as we took a detour in to La Storta to have a look at the cathedral. Outside its closed door, much to our surprise, we met the Germans again. This we were sure would be the last time as they were headed for Rome tonight.

We walked as close to Rome as we could manage and stopped in Ottavia to find a bed. In the first church we went to we met a Polish priest who made it his mission to find us somewhere to stay. We all walked to a convent and waited while the nun went off to ask Mother Superior if we could stay. Message came back that we couldn't; however, the priest had another place up his sleeve. As we got up to leave, the priest, who could tell I was in great need of a bed, refused to let me walk the hundred metres to the next convent and instead insisted I waited for him to get his car. Half an hour later he reappeared and chauffeured me the 100 metres while the boys walked and we all entered through the gates of another convent. Together with Cristian and Claudio I sat on a bench outside what seemed to be an old people's home run by nuns while our friend went in to plead on our behalf. Twenty-five minutes later a welcoming nun accompanied him out saying 'sì, sì'. We shook hands with the priest who refused to take any money and a young man with a t-shirt reading Punk 1985 in big letters across it led us to a locked up building where we were given two rooms ready for visitors and told dinner was at seven.

I showered and lay in bed feeling so on edge. I could either fall asleep or burst into tears. It is five past six and has been the longest day of the whole journey. Despite the knowledge it will all be over tomorrow, the pain of my feet just does not go away. I am excited but I feel much closer to the edge of depression than elation and I wished I had the stamina to enjoy the final night with the brothers.

Cristian and Claudio were in a room above me and at five to seven they came knocking on my door and we headed to the refectory in the main building. The room was full of nodding old people and we had to hold it together to avoid getting uncontrollable giggles about where we had ended up. There was little background noise and the food came and went with hardly enough time to finish one course before another arrived. I got into bed with scarcely a second before I fell asleep, just hoping I would wake with enough energy to live tomorrow to the full.

Ottavia - Roma. October

I woke at five-thirty and could sleep no more. It was dark outside; I said my rosary in bed under the covers, showered and headed across the courtyard to the coffee machine in the main building. It only took thirty cents and gave no change. I put in a euro, happy to feed it too much money in exchange for a very short thick plastic cup of coffee. I sat outside on a bench next to two old people and I listened to their constant chatter as the sky lightened and the stars faded. At six-thirty I returned to the building in the hope that I could hear the brothers getting ready. I met them at the door settling their enormous rucksacks on tired backs. We said goodbye to the nun who stroked my face and kissed me. We all gave her twenty euros, which at first she refused but when Cristian said she could say Mass for us in exchange she settled for that. We headed back to the busy road, quiet with the thought of Rome. It was wonderful to have their company on the greatest day of the whole journey. We walked at great speed like a trio of Indians against the traffic, which was thankfully in accordance with six-thirty on a Saturday morning. We stopped at a patisserie and they went in to buy breakfast. My tummy was digesting nerves and had no space for anything else. They ate croissants on the pavement and on we headed not talking much. What do you say? It is strange to live the day you have thought about throughout the journey. You ask yourself 'What am I thinking and feeling now I am here?' and you struggle to find an answer. The only thing you are conscious of is walking at great speed as if you cannot stop your feet.

We climbed up the steps through the archway into the walled Monte Mario Park and headed on up the winding footpath through the trees until suddenly at the very top there it was, the vast view down on St Peter's Basilica. The sky was hazy with the accumulating heat of the day and we stood as silent as melting ice, just staring at the big round dome dominating the bird's eye view. My reaction was yet to catch up and looking down I felt very little. At the 2080th of 2083 kilometres I got the first glimpse of the place I had been imagining, focusing on, aiming for, longing to get to for the last eighty-two days. For the first time with the thought of it in my mind I did not have a tear in my eye and a lump in my chest. I wanted pure silence; I wanted to look and look and look. It was there and I knew I could reach it, I could see it, and there it was. We moved round the park to a better view and still no words passed as we sat down in silence. The brothers rustled in their bags and out came a patisserie package. They produced three fruit tarts, each of us held one and toasted them and sat on a rocky mound looking down on the great city. I slowly, tasting each bite as if it was the first, ate the most delicious sweet, creamy tart. As one spoke and the other agreed, they said they could not imagine what I was feeling after eighty-two days of getting here as they felt something very special after just five days. I had no answer and smiled instead.

In time we pulled on our rucksacks and, with me leading the way as they recited their rosaries together behind me, we wound down the path through the park. As my boot touched the pavement nothing was going to stop me. I felt as if I was in a trance. My heart beat as if my ribcage was a thick door. I walked with tunnel vision for St Peter's Square. I did not hear anything and took in nothing that I passed. I lived, breathed and felt the beginnings of the intensity of complete peace awaiting me in St Peter's. As the pavement came to a cross-roads the green man lit up again and again as if there was someone else wanting me to get there as quick as I possibly could. My feet and my mind felt detached from my body. We made our way through the streets so as to approach St Peter's up Via della Conciliazione and get the most overwhelming impact possible. Before turning the last corner off Via della Traspontina I stopped and the brothers wrote their addresses in my guidebook. We put our bags back on for the last time and turned the corner. There it was, the most almighty end of the line. Blocking out everything and proving there was no further to go. Set against a pure blue sky it was such bright white there was not a shadow on the ground and I walked as if I had on earphones shut off from the world. I was living the best feeling you could possibly imagine. I was weightless, I could see nothing but St Peter's, I could feel nothing but my pounding heart and a desperation to now get to the square and see some people I knew, some people who knew me, some people who had also lived every single step. Cristian tapped me on the shoulder, I turned around and there they were smiling and said 'You go, go, be with your family.' I kissed them both and went. I walked as if the street was empty, in a straight line through people I did not even feel as I barged between them. I was here, we had done it. I passed through Bernini's colonnade into the space surrounding the Egyptian obelisk and there they were, perched on one corner, looking in every direction for someone they might not immediately recognise but to me there was no one else but them. I flung my arms in the air, my stick went up high, and the tears poured down my cheeks. I could not smile big enough as I walked as if floating towards them. The hugs were enormous, the tears were now tears of complete happiness. I tied my boots to my bag and pulled on some trousers and shoes and we thanked God with a Mass under St Peter's in an intimate chapel of Our Blessed Lady of Czestochowa in the Vatican grottoes. All day I felt on the edge of losing it. I was completely and utterly happy from the very centre. I walked with peace in my heart and belief in my soul.

With special thanks to the London Neurological Department at St Mary's Hospital, Paddington, and of Charing Cross Hospital, Hammersmith; Fr Edward Corbould OSB, and the Community of St Mary's Abbey, Colwich.